Praise for *Let's Stick Together*

"A great book written with warmth and a sense of humour. Full of good down-to-earth advice, it's a must for all couples, whatever age or background."

Rachel Waddilove, author of *The Baby Book* and *The Toddler Book*

"Practical advice we all need on how we can keep our relationships together and have better lives as a result."

David Willetts, MP and adviser on family policy

"There is a desperate need in our society today to equip people with these relationship skills. We have no doubt this book will cause many more couples to 'stick together'."

Nicky and Sila Lee, authors of *The Marriage Book*

"By distilling research into bad and good habits we can all relate to, Harry Benson has done new parents a great service. A former helicopter pilot and combat veteran, he 'gets' how chaps think and act, and communicates couple dynamics with wit and unusual insight."

Dr Samantha Callan, family policy expert

"How much great advice can you get into one little book? Quite a bit if you are Harry Benson. By following these straightforward ideas, you can make a real and lasting difference in your relationship – and at this critical time of becoming new parents. Act on these things and you will stick and not get stuck."

**Professor Scott Stanley, author of *The Power of Commitment*
slidingvsdeciding.com**

"A must-read book both for couples wanting to strengthen a good relationship and couples wanting to transform a faltering one."

**Philippa Stroud, Executive Director,
Centre for Social Justice**

"Easy-to-understand, user-friendly, life-changing information… I wish there were a way to make this required reading for all couples, everywhere."

**Diane Sollee, Founder and Director,
smartmarriages.com**

"Short, to the point, and bang on target. Finally, a book that focuses on the most important issue: how parents can look after their relationship and give children what they most need – secure and happy parents."

**Duncan Fisher, OBE, Manager,
The Kids in the Middle Campaign**

"All new parents should read this book. Its easy-to-follow, practical advice will help you build a great relationship together and give your children the best possible start in life."

**Katharine Hill, Director of Policy Research
and Development, Care for the Family**

Let's Stick Together

Let's Stick Together

The Relationship Book for New Parents

Harry Benson

LION

A Lion Book
an imprint of
Lion Hudson plc
Wilkinson House, Jordan Hill Road,
Oxford OX2 8DR, England
www.lionhudson.com

ISBN 978 0 7459 5399 1

Distributed by:
UK: Marston Book Services, PO Box 269,
Abingdon, Oxon, OX14 4YN
USA: Trafalgar Square Publishing, 814 N.
Franklin Street, Chicago, IL 60610
USA Christian Market: Kregel Publications,
PO Box 2607, Grand Rapids, MI 49501

First edition 2010

10 9 8 7 6 5 4 3 2 1 0

A catalogue record for this book is available
from the British Library

Typeset in 11/15 Caxton BT
Printed and bound in Great Britain by J F Print Ltd.,
Sparkford, Somerset.

Contents

ACKNOWLEDGMENTS 9

ONE   IF ONLY WE'D KNOWN 11

TWO   BAD HABITS 19

THREE   GOOD HABITS 45

FOUR   KEEPING DAD INVOLVED 66

FIVE   THINGS THEY DON'T TEACH YOU
                IN ANTENATAL CLASS 85

SIX   HELPING YOURSELVES STICK
                TOGETHER 112

APPENDIX   HELPING OTHERS STICK
                TOGETHER 119

REFERENCES 123

Acknowledgments

I am hugely grateful to all the people who have helped me get the *Let's Stick Together* programme to where it is today. Alice, Kate, and Nic helped get it going in Bristol. Lovely health visitors and nursery nurses have let us come in and talk to their groups. Cathy, Barbara, Megan, Jo are my brilliant ordinary-but-extraordinary mums who now run most of the sessions. Thousands of mums and dads have sat through a session and told us that they liked it. Richard, Anne, Ann, Siobhan, and John, my trustees at Bristol Community Family Trust, have provided support, encouragement, and wisdom. And my friend and colleague Claire makes our charity run smoothly, arranges all our courses, and has gracefully put up with me in the same office for eight years. Thank you all!

I am also grateful to Lion Hudson for giving me the opportunity to write the book version. Kate has given clear and positive feedback on the various drafts, Julie checked my spelling and grammar (remaining errors are entirely my own), Miranda brought things together, and Rhoda publicized my efforts. I hope this book will encourage discussion of simple relationship principles as a matter of routine for new parents.

Thank you to all the people who have contributed in some way to the content of this book. Amazing researchers give us the confidence to talk about principles that work for most couples and not just me. Generous couples have told me their private stories; I hope you won't mind the new names I've given you! Many friends and supporters have encouraged me along the way in my goal of making top-quality relationship education available to all.

But above all, thank you to my family: my kids, who fill our house with noise and laughter, happiness and love (mostly!); and to my wonderful wife, Kate, without whom this book would just be empty words.

Harry Benson, Bristol, 2010

CHAPTER ONE

If Only We'd Known

In the excitement and utter exhaustion of becoming new mums and dads, the first thing that can get overlooked is your own relationship. The really good news is that for most new parents it doesn't take much to make a huge difference. *Let's Stick Together* will introduce you to simple, practical skills that really work. These principles are based on extensive research but are not exactly rocket science. I've taught them to thousands of people – in antenatal and postnatal groups, in marriage preparation classes, in parenting classes, and in prisons – who have found them incredibly helpful. That's because it doesn't matter how different we are as individuals and couples. It doesn't matter what our circumstances are. The principles of a successful relationship are common to all couples. It's how we manage our differences that really matters. When I remember to use these ideas myself, my marriage goes really well. When I forget, things don't go so well – as you will see! So let's have a look and see how this stuff can make a difference for you too.

Let's stick together!

Let's Stick Together is intended as a quick and easy run through three simple but highly practical principles that will help you make your marriage or relationship the best it can be.

The most important gift you can give your children is a mum and dad who mostly get on, mostly enjoy each other's company, and therefore provide a secure, loving home for your child or children.

All couples are different. But it's not so much the differences that matter – it's how we handle these differences that counts, how we muddle through some differences and resolve others, how we treat one another, how we think about one another, how we respond to one another. What I hope you will get from this book is some really positive and practical ideas for how to handle these inevitable differences.

Family breakdown is often avoidable

Family breakdown is all around. In the UK, for example, 40% of all children will experience the divorce or separation of their parents by the time they finish school.[1] Much of this breakdown happens during the first few years of parenthood. Whether the parents are married or not matters a great deal. Even before they celebrate their child's fifth birthday, 9% of married parents and 35% of unmarried parents will split up.[2]

I think this is shocking. Most parents start family life intending to stay together, yet huge numbers don't make it beyond those first few years.

Professionals and politicians have been telling us for years that family breakdown is one of those things we just have to accept; it's an unavoidable aspect of modern life.

Only that's not true. I have no idea precisely how much family breakdown is avoidable. But what I do know is that it doesn't take much to increase your odds of success. A wealth of research now shows that relationship courses can make a huge difference.[3]

If Kate and I had been on such a course in our earliest years together, I'm certain we would never have got into the mess we did.

If only we'd known...

The things that best qualify me to write to you about being a husband and father is that my wife Kate has put up with me, so far at least, for twenty-three years, and that we have six children. So we must be doing something right to have survived and thrived for so long. But although we now live a fairly normal life of ups and down together, our marriage has been anything but plain sailing.

Our wedding day was a glorious English summer day in June. On such a perfect day, the prospect of anything less than a fabulous life together would have seemed laughable to us. Our marriage was going to be great. And yet within a few short years, we had gradually become more flatmates than friends. Sure, we had a good life and a lot of fun together. But eight years on, and with two young children in tow, Kate confronted me with the reality that a good life was not enough. She needed me to be her friend. And I wasn't. We were perched precariously on the brink of separation.

Within a year of this terrible moment, however, our marriage had become totally and unrecognizably better and stronger than it was pre-crisis. In successfully, and often painfully, working through our differences and coming out the other side, I learned three things:

- The principles of a great marriage or relationship are surprisingly easy to learn, even if they are not always quite so easy to apply.
- Kate and I really should never have got into the mess we did in the first place.
- There are loads of other Harrys and Kates out there who can avoid falling into the same traps we did with only a few small tweaks of attitude and behaviour early on.

Today we have a happy marriage. We're very secure even when we don't always get along. We have utterly fantastic times when we're really close and connected and getting on like best friends. But from time to time we allow work and children to gobble up all our attention, and we start to drift apart. Little things turn into big frustrations between us. When these inevitably come to a head, our relationship feels dark and scary, a little like we have fallen into a crevasse. Thankfully we now know how to climb back out of the crevasse and reconnect again. It takes a lot of willpower but only a little time chatting together to reconnect. Suddenly and miraculously our marriage feels great again. And so the normal cycle of ups and downs begins again, hopefully less dramatic next time round as we spot bad habits earlier and build in good habits more often.

Relationship skills for new parents

Relationship education, as it's called, is still a minority pursuit in most countries. Many couples baulk at the idea of a relationship course. The typical reaction might be "Good idea for other people, but we're OK, thanks." Except that you may not be.

So I originally wrote *Let's Stick Together* as a short introductory session on mum–dad relationships for new parents who had already signed up to an antenatal or postnatal course. *Let's Stick Together* is essentially a condensed version of the best available research on what works and the best available relationship education courses that make a difference. The result is that about one-third of all new mothers in my home city, Bristol, in the UK, are now experiencing some basic relationship education.

I know that a one-hour programme won't change the

world, but it just might make a crucial difference for some. I've already run the programme hundreds of times for thousands of new mothers and fathers, most of whom are first-time parents. Almost all parents – 95% of married or unmarried – found the session "helpful". Two-thirds said they were likely to change their behaviour as a result. A quarter said they were "very likely" to change.[4]

My favourite comments are:

• "The most useful session of our postnatal course."
• "Amazed that the basis of a good relationship can be broken down into such a few points."

The book

In Chapter Two, I will tell you about the four Bad Habits that all of us have to a greater or lesser extent. These habits are not just what I happen to think are important; each of the bad habits comes from world-class research on what distinguishes couples who do well or not over time. I've called them "STOP signs". Maybe you'll find it easier to recognize each other's STOP signs than your own. But this is about your bad habits, what you can do to change things, how you can take responsibility for your relationship, how you can make it work best. The key to this is to recognize that if you want the relationship to work, then you are the one to make it happen. It may be easier to pass the buck and say your other half should do their bit too. It's true; they should. But taking responsibility means not worrying about fault or fairness. Children blame one another. They'll say, "It's not fair. It's not my fault." As responsible adults, we have to break the cycle and make things better regardless of fault or fairness.

Maybe that's too much of a challenge for now. Bear with me. You might find Chapter Three on Good Habits a better place to start. The idea of "love languages" was originally thought up by a psychologist called Gary Chapman. I have interpreted his basic idea and put my own particular slant on it. Love languages really works for me and is probably the single biggest reason why Kate and I have managed to remain married!

Chapter Four of *Let's Stick Together* is all about Keeping Dad Involved as a friend to mum and as a co-parent of your child or children. For many couples, the easiest option can be for mum to take over most or all of the parenting role and for dad to drift into the background. This happened to me a lot, especially with our first two children. I've got much more involved since then. The other key is to make sure you make time for one another. No friendship can survive without time together. If mum and dad want to support each other as parents and friends, then they have to make time for each other.

These three chapters form the core of *Let's Stick Together*. If you're knocking your bad habits on the head, if you're making the effort to love one another in a way that each most appreciates, and if both of you are actively involved as parents in ways that really support one another, then you will both realize what wonderful people you have found in each other.

As a bonus, in Chapter Five I've added a few pearls of

wisdom from my own experience as well as the latest research on what works in family life. I hope you'll find Things They Don't Teach You in Antenatal Class interesting and helpful.

To wrap it all up, Chapter Six is a few pages on Helping Yourselves Stick Together that summarize what you've read. It's an opportunity for you to draw together the things you want to put into action. One of the best ways is to talk to other new parents about *Let's Stick Together*. The Appendix gives you some practical ideas on Helping Others Stick Together, whether with groups or over a coffee with a friend. You don't need to be an expert to discuss these ideas; most capable mums or dads can manage it. Experience is what counts. Relationship education is for everyone.

But first things first. See how *Let's Stick Together* works for you, then have some fun putting it into practice. I hope you enjoy my book.

CHAPTER TWO

Bad Habits

The utter exhaustion of new parenthood means that we don't always react to one another as best friends should. Little bad habits can develop and become entrenched over time and start to undermine even the best of relationships. Four particular bad habits tend to distinguish couples who do well from couples who do not do so well during the early years of a relationship. I call them STOP signs:

S – Scoring points
T – Thinking the worst
O – Opting out
P – Putting down

All parents will recognize one or more of these bad habits. We'll never get rid of them completely. But the trick is to notice them when they crop up, usually when we're most tired or stressed, and stop doing them. Think of them as the seeds of destruction, little indicators of a problem with our attitude to one another. Nipping these bad habits in the bud avoids unnecessary arguments. Little changes now will reap big rewards for our relationship in the years to come.

Watch some short videos of STOP signs at www.letssticktogether.com.

The seeds of destruction

Researchers have long been trying to find out the secret of why some couples do well and others less so. In other words, they want to know what it is that makes love work.

One of the most striking findings from this kind of research is that success as a couple, especially during the first few years together, seems to be less about how well we treat one another and more about how badly we treat one another.[1]

Of course all couples do both. We treat one another both well and badly. We have both good habits and bad habits. We may be caring, kind, loving, and interested in one another some of the time, but we can also be selfish, dismissive, harsh, or aggressive toward one another some of the time. The trick is to do more of the positive and less of the negative. But remember that it's our bad habits that tend to matter most, and those bad habits are most likely to emerge when we're tired or stressed. Welcome to the world of parenthood!

Here's a quick illustration of how the negatives can

take over. Two people meet, get to know one another, fall in love, and after a time get married. Married life starts off as a great adventure together. But as pressures and expectations build, so do frustrations. It doesn't take long for some of the positive things each admired in one another to start to become irritants. They still love each other of course. But they begin to snap at one another over little things. The throwaway comments fired off in the heat of the moment start to have their effect. Although the couple still do a lot of fun things together, the joy is slowly sapped from their relationship. The bad habits have overrun the good habits.

Remember that old nursery rhyme that says, "Sticks and stones may break my bones, but words will never hurt me"? It's a load of rubbish, of course: bones heal remarkably quickly, but your mind may still be replaying the tapes of these hurtful words years later. You are still thinking about that put-down, that dismissive look, that swear word, that little snide comment. It really hurt you. Maybe it was just the heat of the moment. Maybe it was never intended to be as harsh, cutting, and cruel as it turned out. But once it has lodged in the mind, it can be hard to forget.

It turns out that the seeds of our success or failure in the future are present in our relationship today.[2] By analysing short videos of the way couples discuss a difficult topic, researchers have identified four particular bad habits that tend to distinguish couples who do badly from couples who do well over the subsequent years. More bad habits today usually mean more risk to the relationship tomorrow.[3]

I have named these bad habits STOP signs. The good news is that they are easy to spot and therefore easy to nip in the bud. Just like a seed isn't guaranteed to turn into a plant, these bad habits are by no means guaranteed to grow into the weeds that strangle your relationship.

The four STOP signs

S is for scoring points

Someone has a go at you. You feel criticized and under attack. Your immediate reaction is to return fire and point the finger straight back at your accuser. That is scoring points.

"You did this." "Well, you did that."

"Why didn't you do that chore I asked you to do?" "I could ask you the same question – why didn't you?"

"You never do this." "You're not so perfect; you never do that."

Here are a couple of examples of my own tendency to score points with Kate. Like many mums, Kate likes a tidy bedroom and makes sure things get put away. So when she sees an extra pair of trousers or jersey or two of mine left dangling over my chair, she's bound to remind me to make sure I don't leave it there. It's not meant in any way other than a gentle reminder. She likes a tidy bedroom. Please put your stuff away. End of story.

But sometimes things aren't always said or heard so simply. Early in the morning, I'm not often in sparkling form and usually a bit fuzzy-headed. What I hear instead from Kate feels more like an accusation: "You've left your trousers lying on the chair." I see a metaphorical finger pointed at me. It seems a bit unreasonable to find myself put on the spot so early in the morning. And anyway, what is she going on about? I'm usually pretty good at putting my stuff away. I'm beginning to feel quite defensive. But hang on a second... look over there. "How about your stuff? Are you going to put your clothes away?" Before I can stop myself, the words are out. I am scoring points. I'm not dealing with the basic issue; I'm changing the subject. I'm defending myself. In fact I'm even attacking Kate.

This is where the idea of a STOP sign is so helpful. Even in my fuzzy-headed early morning half-awake state, I know immediately that I am scoring points. I know it is stupid. I know I shouldn't have done it. It is like seeing a big red STOP sign in front of my face.

My immediate reaction is firstly to apologize to Kate – "I'm sorry. I'll put them away" – and then to deal with the offending trousers. A little change of direction now, a bad habit nipped in the bud, means we avoid what might have become at best a spat that left a bad taste in the mouth and at worst a monster argument that rolled on for days.

Here's another example of scoring points nipped in the bud. Both Kate and I dislike waste at home, so we often find ourselves turning off lights left on around the house by the children. But the bathroom heater has a special place in Kate's heart as a prime source of waste.

Leaving the bathroom heater on drains both electricity and money.

So one bleary-eyed morning, I find myself quietly brushing my teeth in the bathroom when a voice from next door points out that "Harry, you left the bathroom heater on the last two days". Of course, all Kate means is to remind me to make sure I turn it off because she doesn't like the waste. What I hear is very different. I'm sleepy and my defences are down. Kate's gentle reminder to turn things off becomes a finger of accusation pointing at me. I don't like it.

Now, one of my little preferences is that our bath gets cleaned out after use. It doesn't usually bother me that I appear to be the only one who does it. My wife and my teenagers use the bath but don't appear to share my enthusiasm for a quick tidy-up afterwards. But hey, it only takes five seconds with a shower head. So no big deal – until today.

So I'm suddenly feeling got at. "You left the bathroom heater on the last two days." I happen to glance down at the bath. I'm about to launch forth with my brilliant reply, "Well, you never clean the bath out." Luckily the words never pass my lips. Stop! I realize that I am scoring points.

Once again the gentlest, most sensible route is to apologize. "I'm sorry. I should have turned it off. I'll make sure I turn the heater off when I'm finished." Problem solved. Can you imagine what kind of a day we might have had if I hadn't kept my mouth shut? A tiny change by me avoided a potentially huge argument or escalation.

Some might think it all seems terribly unfair that I'm the one who has to make the sacrifices here. I'm the one who has to back down. Shouldn't Kate bear some of the responsibility? All I know is that I want my marriage to work, and I want the best for Kate. So what if I have to back down occasionally? The truth is that both of us want the best. I know that Kate holds back from scoring points as well. But that's up to her. As for me, I can only be responsible for my own behaviour.

Love and commitment require sacrifice. It's not very wise to insist on winning some petty argument but end up losing the relationship. If I behave nicely toward Kate, she's going to feel a whole lot more loved, and our marriage will go a whole lot more smoothly. If I behave badly just because I've misinterpreted what was a reasonable request, then more fool me.

How to spot a genuine apology

Apologizing is usually the best way to sort out the mess you've made by scoring points. But do you know how to tell a genuine apology from an insincere one? It's terribly obvious, for example, when a politician says sorry and doesn't really mean it. They can look as sincere as they like but you just know. "I'm very sorry that it happened", or even worse, "I'm very sorry that you feel this way." It's not a real apology; it's just an expression of regret. Children are a little more obvious. "Say sorry to your brother." The reluctant answer comes through gritted teeth: "Sorry".

The secret to a great apology is the admission "I was wrong", "I blew it", "I made a mistake", or "I screwed up." Without that additional acknowledgment of doing something that shouldn't have been done, an apology is little more than an expression of regret.

I'm constantly surprised at how some people, more often men than women, seem to find it hard to admit they did something wrong. Pride takes over. "Why should I say sorry? It was just as much her fault." And now we're back into defending ourselves and blaming somebody else – scoring points.

Who cares if it's not fair? It's not a sign of weakness to admit you were wrong. It just makes your refusal to admit it seem stubborn and foolish. It takes a real man, or woman, to apologize. The reason to say sorry is because you love. Look at it from their point of view. If your loved one does something stupid, it's so much easier for you to forgive and move on if they admit they shouldn't have done it. A sincere apology takes the sting out of the argument. So go and do likewise.

The next time you hear an insincere expression of regret, you'll know exactly why you remain so unconvinced!

T is for thinking the worst

Does this ring any bells with you? "He's brought me flowers. What's he done wrong?" Or in a similar vein, "He's being nice all of a sudden. I wonder what he wants." Or, not to be too sexist about these things, "She made herself a cup of coffee this morning but didn't make one for me. I wonder if I've done something to upset her." Yes, I hear from dads who have had exactly that thought.

These are all examples of thinking the worst. You're assuming that behind the harmless deed or omission lies some dark intent to get at you, to gain some advantage, to do you down. The good news is that for most couples, most of the time, thinking the worst is not a fair reflection of reality. Most people aren't out to get one another.

So where on earth does this kind of negative thinking come from? We're not born thinking the worst. The most likely source of thinking the worst is past experience. Maybe our parents were less than perfect in the way they treated us. Maybe a teacher put us down. Maybe it was a past relationship that deteriorated into something not very nice. In each case, when we get used to being treated a certain way, it can become a belief that this is the way people treat us generally. We then take that belief and continue to apply it in a new situation, whether appropriate or not.

Thinking the worst is not the same thing as pessimism. Thinking the worst is misinterpreting something that has happened. Pessimism is expecting the worst so that anything better is a bonus. Pessimism may not be an especially positive way of viewing the world, but it is not as destructive as thinking the worst. Expecting the worst is often justified; thinking the worst is rarely justified.

Now this doesn't mean we have to head off to a therapist to help us deal with the childhood trauma that makes us think the worst. If we are reasonably sure where our "thinking the worst" bad habit comes from, then hopefully we can find a way to forgive that person and move on. But the much more important issue is how we behave right now when we think the worst.

I tend to think the worst. I assume I'm in trouble with Kate unless proven otherwise. It's pretty stupid, isn't it? I'm sure this is my most difficult bad habit to crack. Kate won't agree with me because she can't see the thoughts I'm thinking. But I think it's also less obvious because I'm getting better at dealing with it.

When I think I'm in trouble, I'm going to behave in a way that keeps me away from facing the consequences of that trouble. So for me, thinking the worst is very closely linked with a desire to opt out, to hide, to avoid Kate. We'll come to opting out in a minute. (From my study of 236 new parents, about half of those who think the worst also tend to opt out.) Sometimes my assumption that I'm in trouble is thoroughly justified: I've done something I shouldn't have done, or I've failed to do something I should have done. But most of the time, I'm not in trouble; I'm just thinking it. Thinking the worst puts me on the defensive when there is absolutely no need for it.

How anyone deals with thinking the worst is by talking about it. I have to face my fears and check out reality. I've learned to ask Kate open questions such as "How are things?" "How's it going?" "What's up?" "How's your day been?" "What's on your mind?" If I'm feeling brave, I might even ask direct questions such as "Are you OK right now?" "Is anything troubling you?"

It can feel scary asking these questions. After all, if I really am in trouble, it can be a little like walking into the lion's den! Thankfully, most of the time, Kate simply appreciates the fact that I've asked the question. I'm showing interest in her life. I'm showing that I care. Alas, I'm not always as loving and altruistic as my questions might sound. The added benefit of asking the question is that I'm also checking out that I'm not in trouble. A positive response from Kate makes me feel both relieved and connected – so a double whammy of positives. And the more I ask the question and find out that I'm not in trouble, the more likely I am to ask the question again next time I think the worst.

Asking questions doesn't stop me from thinking the worst. But it does make me more likely to check out whether my thoughts are justified.

Past experience

Past experience, especially during childhood, can have a profound effect on the way we think as adults. Mike and Jessie both trace their own deeply ingrained STOP signs to bad experiences as children at boarding school. Mike learned to opt out because it was the safest way to deal with fear. Jessie learned to think the worst because her parents dropped her off one day and didn't come back for weeks. The problem is that these habits, once learned, become automatic and won't go away. Although this lovely couple probably struggle more than most with their STOP signs, they have also found ways of dealing with them really well.

Jessie: My thinking the worst is to do with events. I see something happening now and assume it will always be like this.

Mike: We spent our honeymoon in a remote part of Europe. It was idyllic. On the third morning as we got up for breakfast, I thought I'd switch on the TV to catch up with the news. I turned around and Jessie was in tears. I think she saw our lifetime together being one where mealtimes would be dominated by having the TV on in the corner. For Jessie, mealtimes are for talking, not TV. Seeing this future seemed really grim.

Jessie: I was thinking, "Who have I married? Is he someone that watches TV every mealtime?" I assumed that, yes, this was what Mike was, and I got really upset. I can see it with our baby Amy with more day-to-day things, particularly in the first year when she wasn't sleeping through the night. She was going through little phases of crying a lot, or there were a few weeks when I was weaning her and she wouldn't eat any food. I thought, "Oh no, she's never going to eat anything. She's going to turn into one of these children that gets an eating disorder. Then she'll die…" It is awful. I think it's very difficult to de-programme yourself when you have something so strongly within you. But it's only being married to Mike that has enabled me to see it, because he'll pick up on it and challenge me.

Mike: The first year of our marriage was dominated by

Jessie thinking the worst and me opting out. On my part, it just took some courage to stop opting out and start asking questions: "What have I done that has made you upset?" "What did you hear me say, and what are you feeling right now?" Just beginning to communicate and clarify: "Ah right, you heard this… Well actually this is what I meant when I said this." Initially it felt very uncomfortable to do the opposite of opting out, to walk toward Jessie and say, "Look, we need to talk about this. What just happened? Because I'm confused. Clearly I've done something wrong. You've got to tell me what it is." But actually, that got easier and easier. The more that we did it, the more we were able to pre-empt the explosion, the more the understanding built up between us.

O is for opting out

Some of us opt out more than others. Perhaps we're having a discussion about something; but the discussion just seems to be going round in circles. Maybe it's becoming a bit heated. One of us then turns to the other and, with a resigned look, says, "I'm not going to talk about this any more. It's pointless. We never get anywhere with this subject. It's always the same." We then disengage from the conversation.

Maybe we just blank or block one another. Maybe we switch off and close our minds to one another. Maybe we throw up our hands in disgust and start walking out. We're opting out.

Opting out is almost always about avoiding conflict. It

seems to affect men more than women on average, though by no means exclusively so. More men than women seem to be uncomfortable with conflict in the home. Maybe it's something to do with male roles and hormones. Men are supposed to do conflict outside the home with other men, to protect the home. Men are not supposed to do conflict inside the home. Maybe the greater physical strength of men means that the consequences of losing it at home are greater for men than for women. Something like that. There's some research to back this up that shows men are less likely than women to escalate an argument into something physical. No wonder the stereotypical man is often described as running off to hide in his cave. I can relate to that!

Some researchers reckon opting out is the number one predictor of divorce. We have a row about money and one of us opts out. Money becomes a no-go zone. Then we have a row about the kids and the same thing happens. We can't talk about the kids. Then it's the in-laws, or time together, or who is supposed to do the washing, or what we're going to do next summer. Every time we opt out, we close the door on yet another issue. Pretty soon we've run out of things we can talk about without arguing or opting out. We've nothing left to talk about. We drift apart.

By far the most common reason given by couples for splitting up is that they drifted apart. You can bet that in many of these cases, the root cause was that one or both partners had a tendency to opt out from difficult discussions.

I'm a fairly typical bloke: when I opt out of a potential conflict at home, I am well aware that I'm trying to avoid losing the plot and to protect Kate from a major escalation. But that's not how it comes across to her. To Kate, it just looks like I don't care. Whatever she is trying to discuss with me doesn't seem important. Worse still, she can even assume my opting out means that I don't think she is important, that I don't care about her.

Being aware of my tendency to opt out has really helped me think about the message I am sending Kate. When I catch myself about to close down or run away, I realize I have a choice. On a good day, I now do my best to hang in there and keep talking with Kate. I might say something like "Look, I know this is really important to you but I'm feeling really got at. I know you want me to talk about this. So please go gentle with me. I'm a precious soul! I'm still here." A little humour and a smile can sometimes take a bit of the heat out of the situation.

Of course, there are bad days when my urge to flee is simply too great. Kate would definitely tell you that opting out is my biggest problem. I hope she also recognizes I'm getting better at facing up to the difficult or contentious issues.

One of the things Kate sometimes does that makes a huge difference to me is to preface a discussion with "Harry, I need a good rant. Don't take it personally. Just shut up and listen!" I can do that – no problem. I don't need to think the worst. I don't need to opt out from conflict. I have even been told how to solve the problem in hand: the solution is just to listen!

Time out is not opting out

Sometimes it's just the wrong time to talk. I'm trying to get some work finished. I'm watching the game on TV. It's late and I'm exhausted. I haven't eaten all day and all I can think about is food. Something happened at work today and I can't get it out of my mind. It's been a long day and I need a drink before I can even think. I've just put the children to bed and I'm feeling really wound up. I just need a few minutes to myself. I can't concentrate on you because I'm too Hungry/Angry/Lonely/Tired (HALT).

In any of these situations, it's perfectly reasonable to take a time out. If I ask for a time out, this is not the same as opting out. The big difference is that I'm not running away indefinitely. Time out has to be followed by time in. I'm going to come back and discuss it in twenty minutes, when I've calmed down, when I've got a glass of wine in my hand, when the game is over, first thing in the morning, when I've had something to eat, when I can give you my full attention.

But in order to show that I'm not opting out and that I do care, I still need to tell Kate what I'm thinking: "I really want to hear what you've got to say. I know it's important. But I just can't listen right now. If we make time to talk first thing tomorrow morning, I can give you my full attention. Is that OK?"

Would that it were this easy! When I'm distracted and don't want to listen, I'm really bad at this. What I do know is that when I use my own version of time out, it does seem to take the heat and frustration out of the situation.

All I then have to do is make good on my promise to chat later... The message is: communicate.

P is for putting down

Think of how you feel when you're driving a car and somebody cuts in front of you. Your whole body bristles with an attitude that says the other person is a moron. You cannot believe that they could be so stupid.

I sometimes catch myself doing this. I might react by saying out loud something like "What an idiot!" or "Can you believe that?" Or I might mutter sarcastically to myself, "Great driving, mate." What I'm thinking is that I'm better than they are; I'm a good driver and they're not; I'm clever and they're fools.

This is the attitude behind a put down. We are putting somebody down when we claim the moral or intellectual high ground and are gazing down on others. We are feeling critical, belittling, dismissive, or contemptuous toward them. Putting somebody down is an expression of our bad attitude. I can get away with it in a car but not with a loved one.

Actually we don't even need to say anything to put someone else down. We can simply roll our eyes, click our tongues, give a sharp outtake of breath, and shake our heads. This is more than enough to show that they are definitely an idiot.

Of course someone can also feel put down even when we don't mean it. They could misinterpret our intentions. Maybe we forget to say thank you or show appreciation for something nice that they've done. They feel put down even though that was not our intent. The main thing here is our attitude toward the other person. We can't make them feel any differently. If they want to feel put down, then go ahead. But what we can do is be aware of when our own attitude is dismissive or critical or, worst of all, contemptuous.

Just once or twice in my married life, I have been in a sufficiently bad or selfish mood that I have felt contemptuous toward Kate. Thankfully I've always realized that this is a really bad idea and stopped myself.

The reason why a put down is so destructive is that you are telling your loved one that they have less value than you. You are invalidating them. It's not a great way to run a relationship. We're supposed to be building each other up, not knocking them down, even if we think they deserve it.

A put down means you need to stop and check your attitude – fast. If you're an eye-roller, then today would be a good day to choose to stop doing it.

Little changes make a big difference

Let me tell you one of the most striking examples of somebody really understanding this. There was a girl called Jane, who I met when I was running a relationship course in a prison. She was visiting her prisoner boyfriend for the day, and I was teaching them and four other prison couples about STOP signs. During the lunch break, I was chatting away to Jane while her boyfriend was making her a cup of coffee. She was very amusing to chat with – very outspoken and not one to hold back on the niceties. But I'm not sure I would have liked to be on the wrong side of her tongue!

She mentioned to me that her boyfriend's coffee would probably taste like bat's p***. I laughed and asked her whether she realized which STOP sign she had just used. She took a moment to think about it but then said it must be a put down. I said "well done" and we continued chatting. A few minutes later the boyfriend appeared with said cup of bat's p***. She then started complaining about how long he'd taken to make the coffee. "He's a nightmare," she said. I laughed again and asked which STOP sign she'd used. She laughed now and quickly recognized her put down.

Well, a week later, I was in the prison for the second day of the course. I was especially impressed that Jane had come back for more, because I knew she had some major issues at home. Her three children, each from a different dad, had all been put into care because of her mental health problems. So it was indeed amazing that she had even turned up. I asked the group whether they had remembered anything from the previous week or even managed to put any of it into practice.

Quick as a flash, Jane's hand went up. "I remember the STOP signs," she said. I was impressed. "Go on," I said. "Well," she continued, "I have noticed that I tend to put people down without thinking about it. I tried really hard this week not to do it. And you know what? My mother told me I was so much nicer to be around."

The secret of STOP signs

The reason I think STOP signs are so helpful is that they rely on only one person making a change. Whether it's Kate or me who initiates this doesn't really matter, as long as one of us does! Kate will undoubtedly be playing her part too. But whether she does or does not isn't the point.

I can only be responsible for my own behaviour, not hers. I can only control my own bad habits and STOP doing them. I can only change the way I respond when I'm tired or stressed, when I'm in a bad mood, or when I'm simply not thinking.

So I don't have to depend on Kate to stop doing whatever it is I don't like. It would be no good me telling her not to score points or not to put down. Pointing out her flaws is simply me scoring points or putting down! I can't make Kate change; I am not responsible for her behaviour, so I should stop trying to do it.

It doesn't take much effort to behave badly. Each STOP sign may only be a little thing, but it can have big consequences. Scoring points can start an argument because I made that little throwaway comment. **Thinking the worst** can start an argument because I'm suspicious something funny is going on when it obviously isn't. **Opting out** can start an argument because I turn my back and refuse to listen. **Putting down** can start an argument because of that tiny roll of the eyes.

If it takes so little effort or thought to use a STOP sign in the first place, then surely it only takes a little effort or thought to avoid doing it. I know this isn't always easy, but every STOP sign nipped in the bud now means one unnecessary argument avoided later. Small changes in my behaviour can therefore have a huge impact on our relationship.

Over the next week or so, pick the STOP sign you most recognize in yourself. You'll find the short videos at www. letssticktogether.com helpful here. Think about the times when you are most likely to use it. Now decide to stop when you catch yourself doing it and see what happens. You never know. Rather like Jane, the mum with whom I chatted in prison, you might be a whole lot more fun to be around!

Nipping it in the bud

Jason and Melissa have a three-year-old and a baby. They are both really good parents, but everyday situations can quickly become flash points and bring out Jason's tendency to put down and Melissa's tendency to score points. This is a really good example in which both parents nipped an argument in the bud long before it got out of hand.

Jason: I was sitting in the lounge at home after work. Melissa and the two children were playing in the hall, just out of sight from me. Piggy backs, horsey rides, that sort of thing. All of a sudden, there was lots of crying. I came rushing round the corner. One of the kids had blood coming from a split lip. My initial reaction was to think, "They are just playing. How on earth could such a small child get hurt playing in the hallway? This is ridiculous." I shouted out at Melissa: "What's going on? Why is this happening?"

Although it pains me to admit it now, I was treating her like an idiot. I was putting her down. Her immediate response was "We do this all the time. It's just normal play. This is what happens." There was more than a hint of scoring points: "You're not here. You're out at work. What do you know? You don't observe this. If you did, you wouldn't have made such a ridiculous accusation." For once, I very quickly realized that she was right. What makes me think I can criticize my wife like this? Do I really have such exceptional parenting skills above and beyond her ability to play with the children? Of course I trust her implicitly as a mum, but some deep-down attitude just comes out. I apologized for my comments and it was resolved almost instantly. Unfortunately I can't say I'm this quick every time!

Melissa: I had no idea he felt that way about the whole incident. I'm really surprised he felt so sorry. It was very sweet of him to say he was sorry and to say he was wrong, but at the time I didn't feel like he was particularly sorry. It seemed begrudging. I felt thoroughly put down. Most of the arguments we have are about the children and follow a similar pattern. To me, the way he reacted was very much a reflection of his disapproval of my parenting. I felt he was putting down my parenting skills. I absolutely hate being told off like a naughty child. It's one of my buttons. So I got very defensive: "You know nothing. I'm a great parent.

You're only here 20% of the time. What do you know?" I responded out of hurt. I said, "When you play this is what happens", as a kind of educational thing.

I was scoring points in my heart because I knew full well that I play with the kids better. You have your head in the computer and you don't notice the fun we were having before the incident. I said it with an attitude that he's a much worse parent: "What do you know about it? You don't play with the kids like I do."

The argument resolved itself quickly for a number of reasons. Both of us nipped it in the bud before it got out of control. He apologized. I realized I could easily get into an escalation. Past unsaid things might have come out. I could have listed all the things he does with the children that I think are ridiculous. At the time I didn't want it to become an argument, which was a good thing because I think it could have been a blinder!

Do you back off or fire back?

When I first started running *Let's Stick Together*, I wanted to find out how STOP signs differed between new mums and dads, and whether there was a difference between married and unmarried couples. So I asked 236 new mothers, after they'd attended a *Let's Stick Together* session in a NHS postnatal clinic in Bristol, to write down how often they and their husband or partner used each STOP sign.[4]

Looking at parents as individuals, there were two fairly unsurprising conclusions. First, all parents have bad habits. Second, men and women are different. It's not exactly rocket science!

- Mums are more likely than dads to score points (62% vs 46%), think the worst (47% vs 33%), and put down (42% vs 20%).
- Dads are more likely than mums to opt out (58% vs 44%).
- The typical mum uses two STOP signs *fairly often* but only one STOP sign *very often* or *not at all*.
- Although the typical dad uses slightly fewer STOP signs, dad uses his as often as mum uses hers.
- In the individual use of each STOP sign, it doesn't seem to matter much whether parents are married or not.

Looking at parents as couples, however, there were some fascinating patterns. The time-honoured strategy of "fight or flight" is alive and well. This is sometimes called the demand–withdraw pattern, where one parent scores points or puts down and the other opts out. It's often linked with relationship problems. Unfortunately it also seems to be quite common. Altogether 61% of new parents, married or not, use some form of demand–withdraw. The stereotype suggests it's usually mum nagging away at dad who runs off to hide in his cave; it's definitely more common this way round. Amongst 45% of couples, women demand and men withdraw. But amongst 31% of couples, it's the other way round: men demand and women withdraw. An energetic 14% of couples manage to do both! This is probably quite entertaining to watch but not much fun if it's you.

But the most interesting, and brand new, finding was there are a couple of patterns that are much more common amongst unmarried couples than married couples.

- "Backing off" is when both partners opt out.
- "Firing back" is when neither parent opts out, but dad puts down, and, in response, mum thinks the worst and also either scores points or puts down.

Nearly half of all unmarried couples use one or other of these patterns compared to just over a quarter of married parents. Backing off and firing back are exactly what I might expect to find in a relationship where dad is a little less committed and mum is a little less secure. This difference in the way parents react to one another is one possible explanation for why more than a third of all unmarried parents, in the UK at least, split up before their child's fifth birthday, compared to one in eleven married parents.

If you think your own marriage or relationship looks a bit like this, remember that backing off and firing back are just symptoms. It may be that the underlying issues have something to do with commitment and security. This is by no means the end of the world. All the principles in this book will help a lot. But you probably need to talk to each other kindly and lovingly about being a couple, an "us" rather than just a "me" and a "you", and talk about your future together. Marriage is usually the most powerful way to say, "We are a couple with a future." But make sure your marriage represents a clear decision about your attitude and intentions toward one another, and not just the easiest option for now.

In my study, I found that almost three-quarters of all the parents who either back off or fire back said they would change their behaviour. I am certain that most new parents can avoid the unnecessary pain of separation if only they are more aware of their STOP signs and nip them in the bud.

CHAPTER THREE

Good Habits

Everybody wants to be loved. Most of us tend to respond best when we are loved in one or two specific ways. These are called "love languages", and there are five of them:

- time
- words
- actions
- gifts
- touch

The problem comes when we assume our spouse or partner responds to love in the same way we do. Although it's easiest and most natural to love them using our own love language, this may not be what they really want. We give love, but they don't feel loved. The secret is to find out their love language and then use it. Once you get this idea, you'll be hooked. It makes sense, it's practical, and it's wonderfully positive. Whereas you can think of STOP signs as the seeds of destruction, think of love languages as the seeds of success. For me, understanding this idea is the reason I'm still married!

We love one another, but we don't feel loved

In lots of important ways Kate and I are pretty similar: we have similar social backgrounds; we have similar personal faith and beliefs; we share similar aspirations for ourselves and our family. But in other ways we are completely different. In fact, a friend of ours recently told Kate she thought we were one of the most unalike couples she had ever met. Did Kate and I agree? Yes and no. Kate said yes; I said no!

All couples are different. Our differences might help you highlight some of your own differences. Our personalities are certainly quite different. For starters, Kate is lovely. Need I say more? To me, her most attractive characteristic is her friendly nature. She is an extrovert who revels in spontaneity and enjoys the company of people. She will easily invite friends and acquaintances, new and old, to come to eat with us or stay. She is always on the lookout for variety and wouldn't choose to have the same experience twice, whether watching films, trying recipes, or taking a particular bike path with the kids. She always has great ideas for the weekend. For Kate, new things are money well spent. Day-to-day management of the household and children tend to be her responsibilities. She is very much a hands-on mother constantly involved with the children. Fun involves spur-of-the-moment excursions to somewhere new. Life is good when there are lots of positives.

Kate would say that gentleness is my area for greatest potential improvement. My strong sense of purpose can sometimes make me more curt and offhand than I intend. I think my main positive characteristic is my sense of integrity and honesty: I try to practise what I preach; I only make promises I know I can keep; and I find it almost impossible to lie. Although I thrive on public speaking, I am an introvert comfortable in my own skin. I love good meaty one-to-one discussions but am not good in a crowded room. I have a touch of the control freak about me, although in a big family this is mostly a lost cause! Nevertheless I like to plan and organize in advance. I book cosy dinners with just one or two couples months ahead. I buy tickets for sports events up to a year ahead. I'm not as good at planning the next weekend, but I am chief organizer for next year's family holiday. For me, experience is money well spent. Longer-term management of money, savings, insurance, tax, and holidays tend to be my responsibilities. My hands-on involvement as a father tends to come in bursts of interest and activity. Fun is a well-planned and executed adventure. Life is good when there are few negatives.[1]

Actually, I think our similarities are far more important than our differences. The similar ways we see the world are the backbone of our life together. Our personality differences are mere shades of colour and subtleties of flavour. Most of the time, these differences make us into a great team. Kate's strengths complement my weaknesses; my strengths complement Kate's weaknesses. Of course, some of the time, these differences become a source of frustration and argument.

But by far the most important area of difference, with the greatest potential to boost or wreck our marriage, is the way we think about love. To me, the most obvious way to show Kate I love her is by giving her a huge hug. Through a hug, I am offering the comfort, security, and warmth that come from the physical connection with another human being. That she will allow me to do this is deeply reassuring.

To Kate, the most obvious way to show she loves me is to spend time with me chatting about life, work, family and other things. Through talking and listening to each other, Kate is showing me that she loves me. She thrives on the connection of sharing what's important, what's interesting, what's working in our lives. When I chat with Kate, she feels loved.

If only it were that easy. What seems obvious, natural, and automatic to me is so different from what seems obvious, natural, and automatic to Kate. Hugs are incredibly important to me but much less so for Kate. Chatting is incredibly important to Kate but much less so for me. If all I ever did to show love was hug and all Kate ever did was chat, neither of us would receive love in the way that makes most sense to us. We could easily get the wrong impression that we are not loved.

It's as if we are trying to communicate love to one another, but we are speaking different love languages. We love one another, but we don't feel loved.

The five love languages

In Chapter Two, I mentioned research that finds that the presence of bad habits is the best indicator of problems in the early years of a relationship. The presence of good habits, however – what researchers call positive affect – can mitigate much of this. Positive affect is when couples display affection, humour, interest, and curiosity in one another. After the first years have passed, the absence of good habits then becomes the better indicator of problems.

This was definitely the case for Kate and me when we went through our marital crisis. We survived the first eight years of marriage because we had a relatively low level of negativity. But over time, it was growing apart through lack of positive affect that took its toll.

The psychologist Gary Chapman reckons there are five main ways to express love. He calls them "love languages".[2] This concept is the simplest way I know to help any couple build positive affect into their relationships. Love languages have been, and continue to be, incredibly helpful in shedding light on how to make my marriage to Kate full of love, life, laughter, fun, and friendship.

The five love languages are time, words, actions, gifts, and touch. This is how I interpret and use them.

Time

If time is your love language, then you love it when a friend or loved one spends time with you. Maybe they just hang out in your kitchen for a coffee. Maybe they sit next to you on the sofa as you watch a film together. They don't have to say very much or do very much. But the message this sends is that they care enough to give you their time. For you, time is love. They could be spending it with anyone else, but they are choosing to spend it with you. Having somebody around therefore makes you feel appreciated, recognized, connected, a valued part of the human race. It feels good. And if time is your love language, then hanging out with your friends is probably the most natural and easy way for you to show love to them. You don't have to do much or say much. You're simply showing that you care because you are there with them. If you can relate to this, then time is your love language.

Words

If words is your love language, then you love it when a friend or loved one chats with you about life, what's going on, anything. It's the communication of information about one another that is important here. It seems so special that somebody would be interested enough to chat with you. The opportunity to share your lives with one another makes you feel connected, valued, special. And if words is your love language, then it probably comes easily and naturally for you to want to chat to others.

It's your way of expressing affection, connection, love. There are other aspects of words that may or may not be important to you. It could be that the way you're spoken to is especially important: gentleness and kindness say everything. Or it could be that being appreciated or affirmed or complimented on how you look or what you've done is especially important: you love being noticed and you probably find it easy to be complimentary to others. Or it could be that encouragement about the future is what does it for you: you are a natural encourager. If you can relate to any or all of these, then words is your love language.

Actions

If actions is your love language, then you love it when a friend or loved one does something for you or with you. Actions speak louder than words. It might be a particular type of action that really emphasizes this. Somebody takes on a chore that you would otherwise have to do yourself: changing the baby's nappy, doing the family shopping, emptying the bin, making the bed, doing the washing up. It could be an action that makes you feel cared for: cooking you dinner, giving you a lift, running your bath. Or it might be a job that makes you feel supported: organizing the car repair or the family holiday, fixing the broken sink, putting up a shelf. Perhaps it's doing things together that makes you feel loved, such as going on a bike ride, taking a walk, or playing sports or games together. It's most likely that the action or activity you appreciate most is also what you find it easy to do for others. If you can relate to any or all of these, then actions is your love language.

Gifts

If gifts is your love language, then you love it when a friend or loved one gives you a little something: a note, a card, a trinket, a chocolate bar, a flower. It shows they've been thinking about you. With gifts, it's very much the thought that counts. It might be rather nice to receive a shiny new Aston Martin and an 8-carat diamond ring, but the love language of gifts is not about the expense. Little is often all it takes. Somebody has spent time thinking about you. You happen to need a diary in that particular format. You'd really like one of those flowers in that particular colour. You could do with an encouraging or sympathetic note. Thinking of others and sending them a note or buying a little gift is probably second nature to you. If you can relate to this, then gifts is your love language.

Touch

If touch is your love language, then there's nothing quite like a hug, a hand being held, a touch on the shoulder, to make you feel loved. There's something about physical contact that conveys love and affection to you; you feel accepted, secure, loved. It helps you feel more open and warm. Touch doesn't mean sex, although clearly sex meets the same need. If touch is your love language, then it's the easiest and most obvious way to convey love: a hug for your loved one when you meet back at home after work, a hand on your friend's shoulder to greet them at a party. If you can relate to this, then touch is your love language.

Men and women are different!

Angela first heard about love languages at a session on Let's Stick Together *in her postnatal group. It really helped her to recognize that, even though she and her husband John share much in common, they are different in the way they show love to one another.*

Angela: Love languages really struck a chord with me. John and I are quite similar in lots of ways. So I've tended to assume that he's going to like the things I do for him, because I like them myself. Since baby David came along, things have changed. Our differences have become much more obvious. As new parents, John and I have less time for each other. So the ways we show each other love has become especially important.

Recently, John went away for the first time since David was born. I'm a gifts person and also a words person. So I especially like giving people things or sending texts that really show how much I'm thinking of them. I assumed John would bring me back something really nice because I hadn't had much in the way of communication. What I got were the biscuits from his hotel bedroom. They were perfectly nice, but I couldn't believe that was all he had brought me. I just said, "Is that it? That's pathetic! I was expecting something really nice from duty free. When you go next time, you'd better make sure you get me something nice."

John's love language is touch. He gave me a big hug when he got home. He was quite pleased with himself as he gave me the biscuits. I was not impressed. It was like he'd just picked them up as a last-minute thought.

Talking about love languages has been helpful. Now I've had time to think about it, I do realize he was thinking more about us than a packet of biscuits. I'd just do things in a different way. Now when he makes a gesture, I know he's taken time out to think about giving that gesture or doing something for me.

Riding the cycle of marriage

It's a simple rule. My own marriage works best when I remember to love Kate in her love language. Things go downhill when I forget!

My marriage to Kate is unrecognizable from what it was before our crisis in the mid-1990s. However, even though we are deeply secure in our commitment and love for one another, the way we get on with one another still goes through a cycle of ups and downs. If you think about this for a moment, then you will realize that relationship cycles are completely normal. In fact, they are inevitable. I reject the whole concept of a stable relationship. Relationships can be secure, but they cannot be stable. They must always be cyclical. Here's why.

When I am being nice to Kate, it's a whole lot easier

for Kate to reciprocate. Her niceness to me in turn makes it easier for me to be nice back to her. And so on. The positives feed on each other. We're on an upward spiral where our marriage feels really good. But when I am less than nice, and especially when I forget to be nice, it becomes harder for Kate to be nice in return. She might not be outright unpleasant to me, but perhaps she becomes a little more closed or resentful. At the very least, she might be tempted to stop being nice. The reaction I get from Kate then makes it harder still for me to be nice. Not being nice to each other puts us into a negative spiral where marriage feels rather less good.

In our case, the cycles seem to be less like a series of waves and more like a series of straight lines. We start off doing really well. We enjoy each other's company. It's easy enough to love each other in our own love languages. Actions and touch are second nature to me. Time and words are automatic to Kate. When we're getting on well, we want to make the effort for one another. So giving time and words to Kate, her main love languages, is a real pleasure for me. Giving actions and touch to me, my main love languages, is a real pleasure for Kate. This is the up part of the marriage cycle and can last for days, weeks, or months.

Sooner or later, however, the challenges of work and family roles and responsibilities cause us to take our eyes off the ball. It's precisely because our marriage is going well that we are able to switch our main focus to these other needs. The urgent and noisy demands on our time begin to take priority over the importance of everyday connection between us. It's the little moments, little words, little acts, little touches, that keep the upward cycle going. And it's these that gradually get lost. It's not deliberate. It's not malicious. It's just that they get forgotten or overlooked.

With every step that we drift apart, it becomes harder to re-establish the good habits that make us such a good team. We can both see this happening. But ironically, instead of choosing to love one another in the way that connects us best, we tend to retreat into using our own love languages more. Perhaps it's an attempt to signal what we really need. Perhaps it gives us an excuse: "I'm doing my best." But neither of us feels quite brave enough to reconnect and restart the cycle. Eventually some little frustration bubbles up to the surface and develops into a full-blown row. The distance and the hurt that come with this makes us realize we have stopped paying attention to one another. We have to do something now: we have to choose to love one another.

I sometimes think our particular marriage cycle is like a journey across the Arctic snow and ice. It's an exciting and challenging adventure together for most of the time but only safe as long as we are in it together and working as a team. Every now and then, we become overconfident and lose concentration. We start to think we can enjoy the adventure on our own. We forget the safety rules and allow ourselves to let go of one another. Almost imperceptibly, we start to drift apart. We are both aware when this happens but try not to let it worry us. At some point it becomes apparent that things are beginning to drift out of control. Still, neither wants to admit it. Other priorities allow us to ignore the growing sense of danger. Our cries for help tend to focus on our own needs rather than supporting one another. Sooner or later some little issue triggers an argument, and we fall suddenly and shockingly into a deep, dark crevasse. It feels scary and alone. Well and truly stuck in this difficult and uncomfortable situation, eventually one of us summons the courage to initiate the rescue mission. It seems like a huge task. Yet the extraordinary thing is how quickly we can get back on track and start working as a team together.

Dealing with our crevasse moments

A few years ago, after our fifth child was born, we were both completely exhausted. I had suffered from pneumonia while Kate was pregnant. This was real pneumonia, please note, not just "man flu"! I wouldn't wish pneumonia on anyone. I was in bed for a month with a high fever. It must have been utterly shattering for Kate to carry the family load while staring at her helpless, bed ridden husband. We were fortunate to be blessed with a wonderful church family who brought meals to us and ran errands for us for weeks on end.

Soon after the baby was born, Kate and I both knew we badly needed time together. We needed to connect. So we were very excited at the prospect of a reunion dinner at a Thai restaurant in London with old pals of ours from our Bangkok days. All the child arrangements were made, and we headed off in our van – we are long past being able to fit our big family into a car – for a lovely evening in London. We thought it would be good to chat on the way there and back.

Only that's not quite how it worked out. Instead, we fell straight into a crevasse.

Soon after we headed out of Bristol, some small issue or misunderstanding – the details of which I can no longer remember – started to degenerate into a full-blown argument. We drove the entire 120 miles on the motorway arguing. Two hours later, we parked the car near the restaurant and stopped arguing for long enough to have dinner with our friends, which was the lovely part of the evening. Late at night we got back in the van and continued the argument all the way back down the motorway. It's extremely unpleasant driving a van when you desperately want to opt out of a conflict – there's nowhere to go. We got to bed at 1:30 in the morning.

The following morning, we got the kids ready and off to school. One of the disadvantages of working at home is that I still couldn't escape from the row. Eventually, by mid-morning, we finally agreed on something. We needed to stop arguing.

We decided to call some lovely friends of ours, Arthur and Jenny, who are a little older and a lot wiser. Jenny answered the phone. "Can we come over and see you?" I squeaked. Bearing in mind that they live 150 miles away in Sussex, our journey to get there might have been interesting. Nonetheless Jenny agreed graciously. But she also seemed surprised that we needed their help. Surely I should know what to do by now? After all, I teach courses on relationships. "But it's not working," I mumbled rather sheepishly.

Just before we rang off, Jenny asked whether I was spending time with Kate. It was like a light bulb going on. I said thank you and hung up. The error of my ways was suddenly all too apparent.

Kate's love languages are time and words. She flourishes best on chatting and kindness of voice. It requires my full attention and eye contact, especially at times when we so badly need to connect. Driving a car or van is the worst possible place to attempt this, for the obvious reason that eye contact is difficult and my attention is divided. It's hard to catch every little nuance. It's easy to misinterpret or misunderstand, which is exactly what happened in this case. And then we fell into the crevasse.

I may be foolish in that I allow our marriage to fall into the same type of crevasse again and again. But I am learning to fall into them less often. And most importantly, I'm getting much better at finding my way back out again. On this particular occasion, after all the kids were in bed, Kate and I sat down together on our own bed and started chatting. We talked for three hours about everything and nothing. Through the almost miraculous healing of time together, we reconnected. Our marriage was back up on the top of the cycle.

Who speaks what love language?

As well as asking the 236 new mothers about STOP signs for the research study I described in Chapter Two, I also asked them which love languages they and their husband or partner related to most.

Almost every mum and dad relates *fairly strongly* to two or more love languages. Most parents relate *very strongly* to two love languages.

In terms of personal preferences, time, words, actions, and touch are equally popular amongst mums, each attracting between 36% and 42% of strong preferences. Only 17% of mums go for gifts. For dads, actions and touch both attract 46% of strong preferences, followed by 28% each for time and words and only 10% for gifts.

So gifts is easily the least common love language for both men and women. Women's preferences are shared equally amongst the other four love languages, but men's preferences are clearly skewed toward actions and touch rather than time and words.

This gender difference is even more obvious when I look at individual couples in which a particular love language is valued by one parent but not the other. Where only one parent likes either time or words, it's more often the mum. Where only one parent likes either actions or touch, it's more often the dad.

These differences are what we might have expected, but they don't tell us much that is terribly useful. Women want to chat a bit more than men. Men want to hug and be active a bit more than women. Great.

By far the most interesting and useful finding from the study is that very few couples share exactly the same combination of love languages. Only about 6% of couples have exactly the same mix. Even then, many or most couples will use each particular love language in subtly different ways, as I explained above. Perhaps more remarkably, whatever love languages one parent likes, in 73% of all cases the other parent won't reciprocate. Put another way, for any one of your favourite love languages, there's only a one in four chance that your spouse or partner will reciprocate!

So whatever makes you feel loved, three times out of four your loved one won't feel the same way. We're different.

Note: Because my study relied on answers from mums only, I wanted to check that they were reporting dads' preferences accurately. So I ran a similar study with fifty-six engaged couples, where I could ask the men as well. Reassuringly, the women turned out to be pretty good guessers over 90% of the time. Somewhat to my surprise, the men were just as good! Both were spot on 50% of the time and completely wrong only 8% of the time.

The secret of love languages

Most people find the idea of love languages incredibly helpful. For me, it has been a key to making my marriage work well. When I remember to use Kate's love language, all is well in the Benson household. When I forget, we begin the gradual slide toward a crevasse moment. The good news is that I can stop the slide and reconnect with

Kate at any moment. The rewards are huge. The price is a little conscious effort, choice, intent, or decision to love in a way that isn't automatic or obvious, especially when I don't feel like it.

It's well worth a really good conversation together to establish exactly what each other's love languages are. Kate's most obvious love language is words. But it's not just chatting that matters to her – it's the way I talk, my tone of voice, my attitude toward her. If I am in any way abrupt or curt, our chatting counts for nothing. It's as if I am putting her down. But if I am gentle and caring in the way I support her and listen to her, I am building her up and showing how much I value her and am interested in her well-being.

Love languages can be very specific and even quite surprising. Strangely enough, words is also one of my love languages, but in a completely different way than it is for Kate. Whereas she loves chatting, I love encouraging others and I love being encouraged. So let's say you meet me after reading this book. Having a chat together would be very nice. Complimenting me that the book is really good would also be very nice. But what would be really special is to hear you say how the book had helped you personally and that you think all new parents should read it. That's encouragement. It's what I tend to do most naturally. I love seeing the potential in other people and encouraging them. Words of encouragement is one of my love languages.

My choice of actions is also very specific. I do generally

enjoy doing things with others. I love organizing events and holidays. But oddly these are not what make me feel most valued. What I appreciate most is when somebody does something for me that I would normally have to do myself. Cooking me dinner or getting my clothes washed are wonderful but still not quite right. What I really notice is if Kate makes my bed or empties a bin, roles I normally take on. Once a year is all it takes. This only became obvious to me recently when a friend of my daughter helped me clear up after a birthday party. He made a big impression on me because I would normally have expected to clear up myself.

Kate agrees that I tend to help others do things that they would have to do for themselves. She notices that I am quick to help with the computing and admin side of her cookery business. She would normally have to do this herself but finds it hard. In the same way, although I am quite capable of working on my own, I have worked for years now with a very special friend and colleague. I think we are a brilliant team in part because we respect each other's different capabilities, and neither of us has any desire to steal each other's thunder. But I know she especially appreciates the way that I am really good at rummaging around doing background research that she would normally have to do herself. It's easy for me because I love doing it. Practical support is one of my love languages.

Because we have talked about this idea a lot, Kate and I have hit on more or less exactly what we need to do to convey love most effectively. I highly recommend that you take the time to work out the exact nature of your love language. We've found this really helpful with our children. One of our teenagers is especially brilliant at making friends. She chats and hangs out with them endlessly. So we, as parents, naturally assume that what she wants from us is time and words. Yet the response to our attempts to chat is all too often a brush-off "whatever". It was only when we asked her what makes her feel loved by us that she replied, "when you play games with me". So her love language turns out to be actions. We still can't get much of a conversation going in the kitchen, but we chat madly when I'm giving her a lift to play sports somewhere.

I recently asked another of my younger ones what makes them feel loved. I expected the answer to be touch, a huge hug. But quick as a flash I was told that we should make something. That evening we booked in for a six o'clock session with the Lego blocks. Bang on time, TV was quickly abandoned and we built exotic aircraft and buildings together on our kitchen table. Later that evening, I was proudly told to look in my office for a surprise. There, perched between two model Wessex helicopters – reminders of my flying days in the Royal Navy – was a Lego airport terminal building. It stays there to remind me that we need to build more together.

The big secret of love languages is to work out exactly what it is that makes each other feel loved – and then tell each other. Don't rely on assumption. Don't rely on mind reading – he should know or she should know. Not true. We won't know unless we tell each other.

It sounds so simple. It is simple. But it's not always easy. Loving one another means leaving our comfort zones and choosing to do something that may not be completely obvious and automatic. The hard part is to do it even when we don't feel like doing it. Don't think for a moment that Kate and I are any kind of experts at this. We're just getting better at it.

CHAPTER FOUR

Keeping Dad Involved

Mum, you're exhausted from lack of sleep, and you need moral support and an extra pair of hands. So you want dad's involvement. But it can be deeply disappointing when it seems like you have to direct him every step of the way. Perhaps it would be easier if you just did it all yourself. If this is you, I have some suggestions – from accepting that a different way can be OK, to biting your lip and letting him make his own mistakes, to remembering to encourage more than criticize.

Dad, you want to do your bit, but maybe it doesn't always work out as well as you'd like. Don't let yourself drift into the background because you get it wrong or aren't sure how to help. The best way to support mum is usually to accept that the way she wants things done is the way she wants things done. She thinks about the baby all the time. You don't. Ask for her advice. Ask how you can best help. Don't take criticism personally. Go with the flow!

Mum and dad, maybe you have noticed how easy it is to drift apart as new parents. New babies are wonderful and beautiful, but they also consume all your time, love, and energy. The single most important thing you can do is provide them with two parents who love and support each other. But no friendship can survive without time spent together. You'll already know that unless you book in time together, it won't happen. It doesn't take much to remind yourselves why you became parents in the first place and that you still quite like each other. Little and often is the key: an hour's walk, a coffee out, telling jokes, having fun together. Book it now!

Mums have a head start on dads

I know I'm not a mum. But if I had a baby growing inside me for nine months or so, my every waking thought would be "baby, baby, baby, baby". Something like that. I've asked loads of mums about this. Everybody smiles and nods knowingly.

All I'm thinking is that if a mini person were growing inside me – moving around, giving off little kicks, making me feel warm in winter and overheated in summer, causing me excitement about the person I can't yet see, making me wonder what kind of person they will become, causing me discomfort at times, interfering with my bodily functions, adding to the sum of things that I hope for, or dream about, or fear – yes, I guess I'd think about them pretty much all day, every day.

But as a dad, I missed all of this. What I saw was a bump

growing on my wife Kate that affected her moods and comfort levels. It made her react in funny and seemingly unpredictable ways toward me. One minute she'd be my lovely wife; in the next breath I'd inexplicably offended her or done something wrong.

The bottom line is that mums have a head start on dads. When the baby finally appears, mums can't help thinking first and foremost about the baby. After nine months of thinking about little else, mums' brains and bodies are automatically tuned in. The baby is going to get most of mum's attention – that's the way it works. It's the number one reason why it's so important that mums stay with their babies in the early months of parenthood. With rare exceptions, nobody else will think about a baby's needs like a mum.

For dad it's a different story. It certainly was for me. Obviously I knew there was something going on behind the scenes. Underneath the bump a baby was growing inside my lovely Kate. Perhaps it's more like waiting to open a Christmas present. What I was really thinking about was that she had a bump. She was uncomfortable some of the time; I was more or less powerless to prevent this. Therefore I needed to tread carefully. And, oh yes, there was a baby in there.

I remember our first. We were in the birthing room of the hospital, being really well looked after. The nurse suggested that Kate sit on a mat on the floor. I was perched on a bed immediately behind her so that she was leaning back on me with her arms draped over my legs.

This was great for both of us because Kate felt supported by me physically. I felt fully involved in supporting her, but, because I was behind her, I was out of the immediate firing line!

My main task was to mop her brow with a flannel and to take little slivers of crushed ice from a bowl and pop them into Kate's mouth. It helped distract her from the pangs of childbirth. As my fingers got dangerously near Kate's teeth, that old Greek legend about Jason and the Argonauts passing through the clashing rocks sprang to mind. I quickly became quite expert at firing small bits of ice from about 3-inch range through the clashing rocks and into Kate's open mouth. My fingers are still intact!

Finally our first baby came out, like a little pink torpedo. It seemed obvious to call her Rosie. I fell in love immediately. She was better than any Christmas present. That initial gush of love was so important for me as a dad, but I hadn't spent the previous nine months thinking of little else. Away from the baby, life, work, friends, and other interests very quickly reasserted themselves, just like after Christmas. My brain hadn't tuned in like Kate's. When I could see the baby, or something that reminded me of her, I would think of her. But out of sight, out of mind. It probably took me about six months to bond properly. This was frustrating for Kate.

So it was Kate who set up the systems, the procedures, the protocols, in bringing up each of our babies. It was Kate who decided how it should be done. It was Kate who decided how and when the baby should eat, play, bath, and sleep. For matters concerning babies, Kate was the boss. I just followed along.

Like most dads, I wanted to be involved. Kate definitely wanted my interest, my involvement, and my support. Two pairs of hands undoubtedly make life a lot easier.

There's a lot of research evidence that being an involved father is good news both for mother and child. Mums are less likely to experience postnatal depression if dads are involved. Children are less likely to have behavioural or psychological problems as teenagers if they have involved fathers, even if the fathers aren't living with them. Perhaps most importantly, father involvement is linked to the quality of the mother–father relationship.[1]

So when I came home from work, I tried to get involved: I would help with changing nappies; I would help with giving my baby a bath; I would do whatever I could to help when the baby woke at three in the morning. But of course, I'm a dad who hasn't always thought things through. When I got it wrong, I usually learned from my mistakes. I learned that putting a nappy on the wrong way round is bad news. It doesn't work. Everything shoots out all over the place. There's usually a rose or teddy or some other indicator that tells you which bit goes at the back. I learned that! I learned that holding a baby in the bath requires a certain posture. Nestle the baby's head in the crook of your arm and hold the baby underneath. It always seemed like a bit of a balancing act to me, especially when soap or baby shampoo is added to the equation. Get it slightly wrong and the baby slides off into the water. Nasty. I learned that! And easing out of bed at three in the morning when the baby is bawling her eyes out is a real act of love to mum. But could I ever master the art of calming the baby down? Rarely. I did learn how to help expunge trapped wind – the baby's, not mine. But most of the time, I ended up handing the baby over to Kate. Whatever I had learned, I was not a mum and didn't have that magic touch.

Now if Kate had been a less lovely person, she might have been less tolerant of my mistakes and said something like "You're putting the nappy on the wrong way round. Here let me do it"; or "You're going to drop the baby. Out of the way, let me do it"; or "It would have been easier if I'd got up and calmed the baby myself." That would be gratitude for you!

It's so easy to see how a tired and emotional mother, whose brain is automatically tuned into the baby all the time, is going to assume that she – and only she – is the expert. Only she can clean and change the baby the right way. Only she can bath the baby safely. Only she can sort out the baby's cries in the depth of the night. Only mum knows exactly what the baby needs. Only mum knows best. It's enough to make a dad feel inadequate or redundant – or so it can seem.

The problem is that mum is also extremely tired. She wants and needs help from somebody she can trust. Dad is very far from redundant. But even though dad offers to help and share some of the burden, mum's brain can't quite shut down and let go of the responsibility. When dad is doing his bit, she's going to be watching him with eagle eyes.

Giving dad a chance

Most mums really want dads to be involved as parents. In our family, Kate loves it when she sees me being involved as a dad. She feels utterly frustrated on those occasions when I don't seem to be making the effort.

Other mums, however, feel much more possessive of their role as the main or only parent. Lisa has always had very mixed feelings about the involvement of her husband Brian. When their two children were young babies, she frequently had to bite her lip when he got involved. "Part of me wants him involved as a father and part of me hates it, feels jealous even, when he does get involved," she says. It was almost as if he was taking away her role as a mother: "Hey, that's my job. Let me do it." She knew it was unreasonable and maybe even irrational.

But Lisa realized how easily she could shut her husband out. Over the years as a parent, she had to learn to overcome her fears and reservations, none of which proved to be founded. The result was that she can now completely trust her husband to be the brilliant and involved dad that he might never have been given the chance to be.

Recently Brian and Lisa were heading off to France for a family holiday. Brian only has three weeks of holiday so this was an important family time. They got to the airport only to discover that Lisa's passport was out of date. A rush of cold sweat overcame her as she realized her oversight and wondered what on earth to do.

Lisa realized she would have to let go of her family for a few days while she got her passport renewed. She knew it would be hard on Brian. They had always shared the responsibilities of driving and navigating their way around Europe. Lisa was worried that Brian wouldn't manage, but even if things did go wrong, she also knew that the children would be completely safe with him. Because she knew what a good father he was, she knew she could trust him totally. All that was lost was a couple of days' family holiday together. What was gained was a reminder to her of the wisdom of giving her husband a chance to be the wonderful dad that he had become.

Mums, don't treat dads like children!

When one of my children doesn't do what I want them to do, it's easy to get cross, pile on the criticism, and generally have a go at them. They don't usually respond very positively to this. Every now and then, I remember that a better strategy can be to bite my lip and let things go, or to sit down with them in a calm moment and talk things through, or to try to remember to spend more time encouraging them and less time criticizing them.

We dads are much the same as children. We don't respond well to being told off like a child. We tend to respond better if you treat us like adults, let us get on with it, and give us a bit of encouragement from time to time.

So if you want dad to do a bit more, or you want dad to

do it differently, here are some questions for you to ask yourself:

- Do I get anxious or annoyed about the way he's doing things?
- Do I get anxious or annoyed because of what he is not doing?
- Do I sometimes think it's easier to do it all myself?
- Do I encourage him to help but am never quite satisfied when he does?
- Does it really matter that he does things differently from me?

If you recognize yourself here, mums, well done. As with all bad habits, this is not intended to give you a guilt trip. It's completely understandable that you seem to be the only one who knows what's best for the baby. It's completely understandable that you are utterly exhausted and probably don't respond as gently and kindly as you might under other circumstances. It's about recognizing the things you do that sabotage your relationships, and then do them a little less. Nip them in the bud.

A lot of this boils down to your attitude toward him. If you want him to be a good dad to the baby and a supportive husband or partner to you, then see whether any of these suggestions ring any bells. Maybe you just have to let him get on with it his way – and that's OK. Maybe he's a slow starter, like me – and that's OK too. Maybe you need to remember to encourage him more and criticize him less. Maybe you need to accept that doing things differently might not be bad or wrong. Maybe you have to let him learn from his own mistakes. Maybe you have to bite your lip and even go into the next room when he's bathing the baby.

Remember that dad wants the best for the baby, just like you. He is an adult too. He can figure things out. He might not do it exactly the same as you, quite as well as you. But that's OK; there are no perfect parents. In any case, babies are pretty resilient.

Do you know how it feels?

A lot of mums have a natural, and understandable, tendency to grab their baby back from their husband at the first sign of trouble. Of course, the message this sends is that dad has no idea. Maybe he does, maybe he doesn't. But give him a chance!

Lizzie, one of the new mums attending a *Let's Stick Together* session in a postnatal clinic, knows exactly how awful it feels because it happened to her. The experience helped her deal with her own natural tendency to grab her baby back too quickly from her husband, William. As she told this story William, who was sitting in on the session with her, showed his appreciation and said thank you to her in front of all the other parents!

Lizzie: A while ago, I was at a friend's house holding her baby. When the baby started to cry, the other mum whipped the baby off me quick as a flash. I felt pretty sad about this! I thought, "I'm an adult. I can do this." That incident has really made me think about the way I treat my husband, William, when he's holding our baby, Josh. I still occasionally have to grit my teeth and even go into a different room. But I really try not to grab the baby off him. I let him get on with it. He's an adult. He can figure it out.

Dads, childbirth is not about us!

Ask me whether I know what it's like to be told off for getting it wrong as a dad. My natural reaction to criticism is usually to take things personally and to shut down. I know it drives Kate nuts that my number one STOP sign is opting out. If there were a human version of an ostrich, that would be me!

Nonetheless, even though I still find it hard, I think I'm getting better at accepting what Kate says about my parenting. My automatic tendency to close down and opt out is still there. But I'm better at hanging in there, hearing what she has to say even if listening makes me feel uncomfortable, and trying to do things differently next time.

The biggest lesson for me as a dad has been not to take things personally. I found this to be especially true when each of our children was being born. Men, childbirth is not about us! I wish I'd known that from the start. During childbirth, I was the nearest and safest target. The way I gently mopped Kate's brow with a warm flannel might have been perfect five minutes ago, but now it seemed to her like I was trying to scrape all the skin off her face. Of course her thrashing about was the pain talking; it wasn't about me. I've finally got the hang of it after six babies.

The importance of not taking things personally is also true of parenting generally. I can guarantee that I find this statement easier to write than to put into practice.

As a mum, Kate automatically thinks about our children so much more than I do. That doesn't mean I don't think about them; it's just that she thinks about them more often. So she may have a clearer idea in her mind of what the children need right now. Thinking about the children is hardwired into her brain because she spent nine months thinking of little else. It's good to remember that.

When Kate tells me something about my parenting, I know I need to listen and to act on it. I don't always find it easy being told what to do. She might not always be right. But that's not the point. If I value her as my wife and co-parent, then I need to pay attention to a subject that is especially important to her because it preys on her mind all the time.

So on the assumption that you, like me, want to be a good dad but are not always in your loved one's good books, here are some questions to ask yourself:

- Do I get involved as much as I could?
- Do I take it personally or otherwise react badly if she tells me I'm doing something wrong?
- Do I find it safer to back off and let her do it all herself?
- Do I tend to get involved only when asked rather than

being more proactive at offering help and looking after mum?

If you recognize yourself here, dads, welcome to the club. This is not a guilt trip. Even if mum sometimes gives the impression that it's better if you're out of the way, it's almost certainly not what she really wants. I encourage you to persevere as a dad who wants to be involved. Hang in there. Make it your business to support mum. Be patient and tolerant even if she gets cross. You might not be doing it right, so don't be frightened to ask questions. You're not born with the knowledge. It's not a failure of your manhood to acknowledge that you could be doing it better. None of this absolves mum from having a go at you unnecessarily. But remember your responsibility. Try it her way. Make it work. She'll appreciate it.

Let dad make his own mistakes (and deal with the consequences)

Amy is another new mum who came to a Let's Stick Together *session. Like any mum, she wants her new family to function as well as possible. Although she is very good at encouraging her husband, Tony, as a dad, she also wants to make sure absolutely everything he does is done the right way. This doesn't give him much of a chance to discover things for himself.*

Sometimes we dads learn better by being allowed to make our own mistakes, even if we have to sort out the mess ourselves afterwards.

Amy: After our *Let's Stick Together* session, I was discussing this with my husband, Tony. He reminded me, very gently, that I have an almost automatic habit of saying "What I do is…" whenever I think something could be done better or differently. Unfortunately it seems I did the "What I do is…" thing almost all the time for at least the first two months after our baby, Nicole, was born. I told Tony how I put her babygro on. I told him how I organize bath time. I even told him how I put the pushchair into the boot of the car so that it would fit. From my point of view, I thought I was being helpful and pointing out the most efficient way of doing things. After all, I had done these things all day while he was at work. Tony told me he felt he wasn't being given the opportunity to learn for himself or enjoy the process as I had done. Without meaning to, I was treating him like a child. Eventually he had enough and told me to stop and explained how he felt. I'm not surprised. We were able to discuss it and now I try to hold back a bit more!

Time: the oxygen of friendship

Before Kate and I had children, it seemed like we had all the time in the world. Spending time together was almost effortless. Let's go out for dinner. Let's go for a walk together. Let's go and play tennis. Let's go away for the weekend. No problem. Let's go. Our main problem seemed to be that we were time rich but money poor.

The ease with which we could freely spend time together meant that staying friends was also relatively straightforward. All I had to do next was concentrate on building my new career in business, and we would be both time rich and money rich. And then we became parents!

Becoming parents completely changed both our priorities and our opportunities. I became much more aware of my responsibility to provide for my family. The success of my career became ever more important. I also became much more aware of my vulnerability. I was more careful crossing the road. Meanwhile, Kate effectively put her cookery-writing career on hold in order to concentrate her energies on looking after the baby.

As we fell into the traditional roles of dad as provider and mum as homemaker, overnight we became time poor. Time that we had previously spent freely together was now taken up either looking after the baby or resting after looking after the baby. If I were to pick a moment when our marriage started to go astray, this would be it. It was barely noticeable at first, but drifting apart is like that. It was only three years later that we hit the crunch point and Kate confronted me. I hadn't really noticed the drift until we were in trouble. I never saw it coming.

Think about time together as the oxygen of friendship. Without time, no serious friendship can survive long on any meaningful level. I am completely certain that had I made it more of a priority to spend regular time with Kate from the start, we would never have got into the mess we did. I've already talked about this in previous chapters so won't labour the point further. But there are some lessons we've learned about time together that may help you avoid repeating our mistake.

Being husband and dad

*Pete and Carrie are a young couple in their early twenties who
have twins. Although the twins were allowed home from hospital
three days after their birth, Carrie was taken into intensive care
for a week. Here's what Carrie told me later.*

Carrie: While I was in hospital, Pete had to look after the
twins on his own, feeding them, bathing them, changing
them. I'm so proud of him. When I got back, it was like they
didn't know me. One of them starts crying. I don't know
why. "It's just feeding time," says Pete. We're very lucky.
We now give the twins to their grandparents once a week.
I really look forward to it. We eat silly things like fajitas. It's
time for us together.

Making time for each other

First, be intentional about your time together. In other
words, plan it in or it probably won't happen. You may be
one of those couples who are naturally good at making the
most of every opportunity spontaneously. Maybe you walk
into the kitchen and your other half is relaxing in a chair.
Your natural reaction is to sit down next to them, quickly
setting to one side the other things you were planning to
do. Other things can wait. Maybe you're like that. Kate
is brilliant at being spontaneous; I have to think about it
more. When I have a plan in my head, I tend to stick to
it. Although I'm now better at the spontaneous bit, I'm
best if I make a plan. So I book an evening with Kate in
the diary.

Second, prioritize your time together. If you make a date to go out together, treat it as you would any other invitation or event. If a better offer comes up, don't change your plans unless you have discussed it and agreed to it. It may be fine. It may not matter much if you miss one evening out together. But it will if this becomes a habit. Let's say you were going to go out for a quiet dinner but your mates ask you out to the pub. If you accept unthinkingly, what are you saying about your time together as a couple? Time together is less important. That's the message you may be sending if you don't treat your time together as more important than anything else.

Third, use your time fruitfully. Everybody wants to know somebody is listening to them. Bad or erratic behaviour, whether by adults or children, is very often the natural consequence of not feeling heard or understood. I'm not excusing bad behaviour; I'm just linking the two events. So when you head off to dinner together, are you excited by the prospect of a good chat? Do you view it as a chance to catch up with your best friend, or is it likely to become a tense evening punctuated by embarrassing silences? Time together is a chance to find out what it's like to wear the other person's shoes. That's what friends do. Ask how things are, what you're loving doing, what you're hating doing, what's on your mind, what you're worrying about, what your hopes and dreams are. These are the sorts of open questions a best friend might ask if they want to understand what it's like being you.

Four, get rid of distractions. The best gift you can give

your children is mum and dad together. It's a whole lot harder being a parent on your own. It's a whole lot easier if you have two pairs of hands and can support one another. The kids benefit from the extra time and resources that you can give them. And of course mums and dads benefit children in different ways. So if you've got a good thing going together, keep it going together for your own sake and for the children's. This means making your time together mean exactly that. If you don't feel comfortable about leaving your baby just yet, then wait until they are asleep and spend the evening in the bath or garden or bedroom where there are few outside distractions. Switch the phone off and let voicemail do the work. If you choose to sit in your living room, switch the TV and computer off. If you go out, get a babysitter, such as a friend, another parent, your mum, or a neighbour. Don't answer the phone unless it's from home. Phone calls can wait. Your world is each other. Don't allow yourself to be distracted.

Five, have fun together. Mums, I really do understand the huge need to talk about the baby. It's completely OK and important for you to do that. But remember that your brain is tuned into thinking about babies in a way that dad's brain is not. I also really understand that time together can be an opportunity for both of you to discuss some of the day-to-day things you haven't had time to discuss otherwise. May I warmly encourage you to remember that your goal should be to have fun together as well! Tell each other jokes. Make each other laugh. You had fun together before you became parents. Have fun now.

Six, go away together. Every year, Kate and I try to disappear for at least one night away from home and the children. Some years we've managed a whole week away. It takes a bit of forward planning. We either have to invite friends and grannies to stay or we have to farm the children out to various other families. But if we can do it with so many children, anyone can. We find these times together are completely invaluable. Even if we've been drifting a bit or going through a bad patch of misunderstandings, it seems to take very little to reconnect. Within the space of just a night away, we remember that we still quite like each other! Nor does it need to cost much. A nearby hotel will do, although a longer trip away may be more fun. Our children occasionally groan when they hear about our plans. The older ones worked out long ago that some of the younger ones are the result of these trips away. But they don't really mind because they know that mummy and daddy time is important for them as well. Maybe it's the sweets we bring home afterwards.

CHAPTER FIVE

Things They Don't Teach You in Antenatal Class

There are a few central principles that Kate and I have used over the years to make life in a big family a bit more manageable and full and a bit less chaotic and out of control. Most of these principles are grounded in solid research findings and complement the three ideas – STOP signs, love languages, and keeping dad involved – covered in a *Let's Stick Together* session. But you probably won't hear much about these in your antenatal class! Maybe you think you should. See what you think.

The best parenting advice ever

Research consistently finds that children tend to do best when their parents provide them with both love and boundaries.[1] But that's not what I want to tell you about!

The best parenting advice ever is this: get a family quote book. Write down the funny little things that children say and adults forget. That's it! Kate and I have been running a quote book for fourteen years now and are forever grateful to our friends Nicky and Sila Lee, pioneering authors of *The Marriage Course* and *The Parenting Course*, for this brilliant idea.[2]

The Benson family quote book is now overflowing with oddities, insights, and pithy wisdom that can only come from the mouths of children. As well as comments, there are also odd writings: such as the angry Post-it note found pinned to our bedroom door that declares "dad you are a idiot"; and the slightly inappropriate letter to the Queen in the year when her mother and sister died, "I hope nothing else goes wrong". The quote book makes us laugh a lot and is our most treasured possession as a family. Should the house burn down, all of our children know that the one and only object to grab in the rush to escape is the quote book.

Once or twice a year, some comment will trigger a rush to the bookshelf by one of the children during dinner: "Listen to what I said when I was five..." Thence flows an unstoppable stream of funny comments followed by inevitable eagerness from the other children to read out their own eclectic contributions. Some of the longer quotes instantly render our whole family speechless with mirth but would lose a lot in translation to outsiders. Here's a selection that might make you chuckle:

- Seven-year-old: "Put my cup in the dishwasher." Five-year-old: "Do it yourself, I'm not your slave." I blame the parents.
- Two youngest children are fighting over use of the guitar. Five-year-old says he picked it up first. Three-year-old pauses before delivering his knockout argument: "I picked it up second."
- All is unusually quiet at the Benson breakfast table. Four-year-old, from behind large cereal packet, suddenly asks eight-year-old, "What's the number in S and N?" "N," comes the reply. "No, S." Long pause. "You are the weakest link, goodbye."

The second-best parenting advice ever

No, it's still nothing to do with love and boundaries, although they remain the keys to successful parenting.

The second-best parenting advice ever is this: establish family rituals. You probably already have plenty of things that you used to do in your family when you were growing up. Whether you call them rituals or whatever, they are the way your family does things, for good reason or for no reason at all. The whole point about rituals is that they give you a sense of bonding and belonging together as a family. They are important for your security and sense of who you are. Family life without rituals wouldn't be quite the same. As mum and dad, you will both have different ideas and expectations about rituals based on your own different family experiences. That's great. Now that you've started your own new family, invent a new set of rituals.

Here are some of the rituals we have built up in the Benson household over the years. First, we have birthday rituals. Seven out of the eight Benson birthdays occur during school term time in the first few months of the year. Because it's usually a school day, all eight of us get up extra early at 6 a.m. and cram into mum and dad's bed to open cards and presents. Much laughter and mess ensues. Somebody usually brings up a well-worn comment from previous years about unbrushed teeth: "Everyone round me reeks!" Then we head down to a breakfast of a teetering pile of pancakes and maple syrup. The birthday girl or boy sits in their special birthday chair decorated with streamers and balloons at the head of the table. They have to wear their special birthday crown. Crowns vary considerably in artistic skill, beauty, flamboyance, and degree of difficulty. Encouraging the children to help prepare the crown and chair the night before has become less of a challenge over the years as the children get older and take on roles without the need for a liberal dose of parental encouragement. But birthdays wouldn't be the same without this whole rigmarole.

We also have holiday rituals. Every summer we spend a week camping at a wonderful family festival called New Wine. The kids love it. We've been going every year for twelve years. Even Kate, who would not normally choose to spend her holiday in a tent, actually enjoys it in spite of the rain and mud. We also spend two weeks in the summer at what we call granny's beach, courtesy of a very generous granny who has a holiday flat. The flat is tiny, best suited for two people. But we cram in all six children on the floor, into cupboards, under sinks, anywhere there is a space. It's little more than indoor camping, but it's great fun and we wouldn't miss it for the world. The one year I messed up on booking dates early enough caused a major family crisis. Summer isn't summer without New Wine and granny's beach.

Another ritual is our holiday scheme designed so that each individual child gets some special time away with mum and dad on their own. Our scheme, inspired by a newspaper travel article, works so that each child gets a week on their own with both parents during the year in which they are thirteen and again when they are eighteen. The idea is to top and tail the teenage years. We've worked it so that Kate and I don't have more than one of these in any given year. It takes a lot of planning but the memories are fabulous. Our thirteen-year-olds have so far sailed in Turkey or bicycled through Eastern Europe. Their choice. At the time of writing, we are thinking about kayaking in Spain with the next thirteen-year-old and heading off to India with our first eighteen-year-old.

As with most families, our particular Christmas rituals are very important. We have our own way of doing things that is probably similar to the way many other families do Christmas. But they remain vital rituals. We buy our tree in mid-December and decorate it from the supply we keep safe during the year in three big baskets. We leave empty stockings or sacks at the end of each bed on Christmas Eve. We all gather early on Christmas Day to open the full stockings on the parents' or grandparents' bed. It is chaos but essential chaos. We rush through breakfast and church and then there's more organized chaos of present opening under the tree, with parents desperately trying to write down who has what from whom for the benefit of subsequent thank-you letters. Eventually we sit down to a vast helping of turkey and all the trimmings. Goose might be a delicious alternative but for us it has to be turkey. The rest of the day is a blur of playing with presents, watching TV, and reheating leftovers for dinner. If we didn't do these things, our children would be mystified. Christmas wouldn't be quite the same.

And then there are individual rituals from each parent. Some rituals have been tried and abandoned. For some years, I ran a dad's breakfast on Saturdays, where dad takes one child out for the morning. Mum soon got jealous, or maybe just hungry, and quite rightly demanded a mum's breakfast as well. This got too complicated and degenerated into what we have now, which is an occasional family breakfast at a particular restaurant we really like.

A dad's ritual that has lasted has been to write a two-page love letter to each child on Valentine's Day, rolled up and tied in a scroll with a red ribbon. My eighteen-year-old has just received the collected *Letters from Dad* printed in a specially bound book. It's a fun record of what she was like over the years. A less formal yet important mum's ritual, on days when Kate has to leave very early to set up a cookery course, has been to gather up the younger children in their pyjamas early in the morning and give them a hot chocolate in the kitchen.

We don't do fair

Something else that unites us as a family is our family mottos. I once answered the door to a friend of ours. As we wandered together into our kitchen, he watched a seemingly unattended four-year-old carving up slices of cucumber with a large kitchen knife. This was perfectly safe because the knife is sharp and cuts easily, and the four-year-old had been well coached by cookery teacher mum. But that's not what it looked like to him. "Ah yes," said our friend, a natural history expert. "I recognize the scene. Big family syndrome. Adapt or die!" And so the Bensons acquired an amusing new family motto and tongue-in-cheek answer to queries about how we cope with big family life. "Simple," we say. "Adapt or die!"

But there is one family motto we've used for years that is both challenging and educational: "We don't do fair." All our children know and accept this motto, even if at times it seems unfair (which is the whole point). Here's why.

In a big family, it is very tempting for the children to compare themselves with their siblings. This is rarely helpful. "He's got more sweets than me" (and he probably has). "She's allowed to go to bed later than me" (and she probably is). "What about me? It's so unfair!" And it is unfair. But we don't want the children to think in terms of fairness at all. Fairness makes them worry more about what they don't have rather than appreciating what they do have. Children don't often compare themselves downwards with those who have less. They only compare themselves upwards with those who have more. A focus on fairness can become a recipe for selfishness, anger, and tantrums.

Anyone who thinks that fairness is important in relationships is destined for a hard time. The reason is that unfairness soon becomes the main issue. Not only does constant monitoring for signs of unfairness waste a great deal of energy, but it also moves the relationship priority away from "we/ours" toward "you/yours" and "me/mine". If you think things are unfair, why would you give without expectation, why would you forgive before receiving an apology, why would you sacrifice without anything in return, why would you take responsibility for sorting out problems, why would you be the one to break a negative cycle? Fairness makes it easy to justify blaming the other person rather than take responsibility for making things work.

Politicians often cite fairness as a core value, but this is also foolish. Adults may be better than children at noticing unfairness amongst those less privileged than themselves. Fairness appeals when looking downwards. But adults still behave like children when looking upwards at the apparent unfairness of those with more. This can lead to envy, an unhealthy sense of entitlement, and, in extreme cases, crime.

Any time our kids start to complain that it's not fair,

they know we will poke fun at them. "WAM," we say, meaning, What About Me? "It's because we love her more than you," we say while trying to keep a straight face. Our aim is always to challenge and never to humiliate. "Oh Mum/Dad," they usually reply as they realize what they've done.

Of course as parents, Kate and I do try to treat our children as equally as possible. But children are different and need to be treated differently. And we are also fallible and frequently get it wrong. It's impossible to be consistently fair. The much better way is to try to do justice and equality. We just don't do fair.

Ask not what your wife can do for you...

Years ago I remember reading a book on marriage in which the author provocatively suggested that any long-term family problems were the husband's responsibility to sort out.[3] I was deeply challenged by this suggestion. Why me? Why not Kate?

Over the years, I've really bought into this wise idea. I see it as primarily my responsibility, not Kate's, to make sure our marriage works as well as it can. I'm not taking anything away from Kate. She has to do her bit too, which of course she does. But that's for her to decide. My responsibility is to do my bit without depending on Kate.

I agree that all this could so easily seem unfair. It could seem like a licence for a badly behaved wife to trample all over a well-intentioned husband. But if his actions make her feel loved and secure, why on earth would she? She won't.

It's really very simple: I want our marriage to work, so I need to take whatever action is necessary regardless of whether or not Kate is doing her bit. The result is that Kate feels loved, valued, and cherished. Our marriage works. We both win.

How foolish I would be to sit back and wait until Kate starts sorting out whatever problem it is. What if both of us take this self-centred and proud approach? Our marriage wouldn't last long. Taking responsibility also helps me avoid excusing myself, blaming Kate, and pointing the finger. Since I can't change what she does but I can change what I do, it is surely more constructive that I concentrate on my own good and bad habits. Both STOP signs and love languages are really helpful here. The buck stops with me.

A young relation of mine was telling Kate and me about some misunderstandings he was having with his lovely new girlfriend. To him, she was behaving irrationally. Kate and I both suspected she was simply crying out for attention, even if she showed it in a funny way. So we talked him through some of the ideas in this book and told him it was his responsibility to make things up with her. He looked at us quite astonished. "What about her?" he said. "She should do her bit too." "I agree," said Kate. "But if you want the relationship to work," she said, "then why wait? You do whatever it takes, regardless of what she does or doesn't do. Think about STOP signs and decide to do them a bit less. Show you love her in her love language regardless of how you feel or whether she deserves it. That is love. She'll notice the change soon enough and will start to feel valued and appreciated. Her love will come flooding back to you." They have just got engaged.

I think that if a man aspires to be the leader of his household, real leadership is all about taking responsibility for both family well-being and family problems. I really enjoy this responsibility and take it seriously. If our marriage is not working as well as it should, it is my responsibility to sort it out.

I'm not saying any of this is easy. It's just rather more fruitful than whining and blaming. Think JFK: ask not what your wife can do for you; ask what you can do for your wife. I think most women would vote for that.

What is a dad for?

It used to be the case that dads went to work and mums stayed at home. Dad was the provider; mum was the carer. Simple. But since the 1960s, mums have had ever more opportunity to work just as much as dads. In more than half of all UK families with children under five, both parents now work.[4]

The interesting thing to me is that this hasn't led to a role reversal. Very few dads stay at home while mums work. In fact the old traditional roles are alive and well. Amongst families in which only one parent works, eleven times out of twelve it's the father who is the provider.[5]

And amongst families who split up, nine times out of ten it's the mother who acts as primary carer.[6]

What seems to have happened is that the role for mums has increased while the role for dads has been diluted. Mums undoubtedly face a great deal of pressure to leave their children in childcare and often experience a great deal of guilt when they do go to work. In case it helps you make your own choice in this, the best research suggests the effects of childcare amongst children under three are both mixed and modest.[7] Some children do slightly better in their learning. Some children have slightly more behavioural problems. And group childcare tends to make this slightly more likely. If mum and dad are content and able to be better parents because they both work, maybe that's more important. You decide.

Dad's problem is different. The fact that almost all dads work suggests that even today dad still sees himself as the provider. Yet if mum works, he is no longer the main provider. And if he and mum split up, the welfare state removes the need for him to provide at all. So what is the role of a dad, other than to be a spare pair of hands to take the pressure off mum?

Here's one idea. I have always thought my main role as father is to give my children a sense of mission. This doesn't mean forcing them into a career box. But then our problem today is not too few options; it is too many. How many young adults finish school wondering what on earth to do with their lives? A sense of mission means getting our children to think about what they want to do with their life, channelling them into a direction that makes sense. This is an ideal role for a father.

When I was a teenager, I always knew I wanted to be a pilot. One of the best things my stepfather ever did for me was to introduce me to a friend of his, a Royal Navy captain, who encouraged me to consider a career as a navy pilot. I did exactly that because my stepfather took on the role of a father and helped me to narrow my own choices.

How do I do this for my own children? Well, at home, I often talk with the children about what they are good at or what they enjoy. These usually amount to the same thing. Even our littlest ones talk a lot about what they'd like to be when they grow up. "Big" and "six" are the answers I have most enjoyed over the years, preserved through our quote book, of course!

Some children, like me, seem to know intuitively what they want to do. My eldest daughter has always known she wanted to be a doctor and probably a surgeon. So my role has been an easy one – to encourage her and help her make connections, to talk to surgeons, find out what they do, and watch them at work. Kate helped organize some work experience. So I'm not claiming exclusivity in this role. I'm just taking responsibility to make sure it happens.

Other children may be less clear about their future. Often a father can see a child blossoming in a role that the child does not yet identify with. It seems obvious to me that one of my children would make a brilliant sports journalist, following in the footsteps of her grandfather. She has the skills, the temperament, and the opportunity. She thrives across a broad range of sports, both playing and watching. She knows I think this. We had a long chat about it on a walk in the countryside when I knew she was listening. But I don't go on about it. I am not forcing her to do it. In fact she currently seems more interested in becoming a TV presenter. Great. At least she is thinking ahead. I am merely here to help her narrow her options. What she ends up doing is her own choice.

As well as future surgeons and sports writers, we have engineers and pilots in our family. Maybe. Of course it doesn't matter if the plan doesn't work out. Of course they can change direction. But having a goal at which to aim provides focus, direction, confidence, opportunity, drive.

And there's one other advantage of dad taking on this role. Giving the children a sense of mission gives dad one too.

Are you a slider or a decider?

Some friends who live a few doors down our street rang me recently to ask whether they could borrow one of our tents for an overnight stay at a party. The wife was rather more excited about this than her husband. So when I knocked on his door soon afterwards, he looked rather disconsolate as I handed over the large green bag containing the tent. "Not a great camper?" I asked. "Hate it," he replied, "but I suppose I'll just have to engage with it and then it'll be fun."

What he was acknowledging was that his enjoyment of the weekend depended on him making the decision to enjoy it. Without that decision, he would be going along reluctantly and would almost certainly not enjoy himself. To slide into the weekend would make the party hard to enjoy. To decide to get into the spirit of things would make the party fun. He made his decision. They had a fun weekend.

I can really relate to his dilemma. If Kate asks me to do something I'm not sure about, and I feel like I'm being dragged along, I know we're not going to have much of a fun time. But as soon as I decide to engage with Kate's plan, I know we'll have a ball.

This idea of sliding or deciding seems especially important to men, more so than women, when it concerns the key stages of a marriage or relationship. It's easier for men to go along for the ride without ever really committing to anything more. The problem is that the further you go, the harder it gets to back out.

Some new American research shows that, even five years into married life, men who had previously cohabited before getting engaged had consistently lower levels of commitment compared to similarly married men who had not cohabited before getting engaged. The married women tended to have similarly high levels of commitment that seem largely unaffected by the order of events.[8]

What's thought to be going on here is that a man who slides into a living arrangement with his girlfriend may not be quite as committed as she assumes he is. But once they have moved in together, inertia means it is harder for him to back out again. He can "slide" in, but he has to "decide" out. Then she gets pregnant because all seems well. But he finds himself ever more deeply trapped. The prospect of twenty years of unplanned parenthood forces him to run for cover. It was good while it lasted, but he hadn't signed up to this.

Commitment is a decision

Lack of commitment from men is one of the most likely reasons why one in three sets of unmarried parents split up before their child's fifth birthday. Men and women may well have different expectations and levels of commitment.

Simon and Anne's story illustrates this painfully but also beautifully. When they met some years ago, it was love at first sight. Their relationship blossomed quickly, and although they didn't move in together, they did spend a few nights together. Anne was delighted when she got pregnant because it was obvious to her that she and Simon were destined to spend the rest of their lives together.

Alas, Simon viewed the pregnancy rather differently. He had never had plans to marry Anne. Indeed, during the few months of their romance, marriage had never even crossed his mind. Although Simon somehow managed to run a modestly successful business, in his own words he was a "commitment-phobe" who drifted from relationship to relationship, "from disaster to disaster", without ever having much of a plan of what would happen next.

When she told him she was pregnant, Anne was

devastated to learn that Simon wouldn't move in and get married. Because she loved him so much and had such a clear sense of their future together, she had wrongly assumed he felt the same way about her. Anne went ahead and decided to have the baby on her own, in the naïve hope that Simon would somehow see the light and find a way to draw their separate lives together. Matters were not helped when Simon drifted back into a relationship with a former girlfriend. The result was confusion and anger.

Things got worse. Throughout the next two years, although love and kindness were never very far away, Simon and Anne fought over access to their child. During a miraculous period of relative calm, Anne persuaded Simon to come on one of my one-day relationship courses to see whether there could ever be hope for them. The course covered STOP signs and love languages and several other helpful principles, including "sliding and deciding".

What they learned that day confirmed what they had suspected: they were good for each other in so many ways. But they found they could relate most of all to the sliding and deciding idea.

They asked to meet me again a few days later. Anne's warm words and body language toward Simon strongly suggested she was open enough to give him a second chance. But it was also clear that this window of opportunity wouldn't last long. Whereas the core problem for most struggling couples is usually a bad attitude, their problem was all about a decision – his decision. Simon had to make a clear and unambiguous commitment to their future together.

It was now or never.

Another week later, I was absolutely thrilled to receive a letter from Simon. He told me that he and Anne had got engaged and had fixed a date for their wedding in the immediate future. After a lifetime of sliding, Simon had finally decided.

Are you a couple with a future?

You may be certain of your own level of commitment, but do you really know how committed your loved one is? How can you be sure? What are the signs to look for? How can you demonstrate your commitment?

I know beyond all reasonable doubt that Kate is deeply committed to me. There are many reasons for this. But you may be surprised to hear that the least important of these are that we have children together and that we share a house together.

To illustrate why having children and living together for years are not enough, consider a couple I know who had been married for fifteen years and had three children. They came to see me soon after the wife found out that her husband had been having an affair. Newly separated, they wanted to discuss how to make their marriage work again. When I asked them to describe their early years together, the husband revealed that he had felt unable to resist the pressure from family and friends to get married. His wife was astonished to hear that he had spent the first six months of their marriage wondering whether he had made the right choice. She had absolutely no idea he had been in such turmoil. He was able to have an affair later on because, in his own mind, he had never made the decision to commit in the first place. Their only hope of a future together clearly rested on whether he was prepared to make that clear decision for the first time now, even if years late.

So back to the question: how can you really know whether somebody is committed? To find out, it helps to distinguish the two different types of commitment. I draw especially on Scott Stanley's fascinating and helpful work here.[9] One type of commitment is the inner bond between a couple, called dedication, that brings fun and friendship. The other type of commitment is the outer bond, called constraints, that makes it harder for a couple to leave one another. Constraints are anything or anyone that views two people more as one couple than as two individuals. Friends, family, and children all see two people as a couple. Being married, living together, having a home, shared finances, and shared history, all add to the picture of two people as a couple.

But dedication is really the key to a successful and secure relationship. Think of dedication like a fire. If dedication is strong, the fire is burning brightly and constraints feel positive. It feels good being married and having friends. But if dedication is weak, the fire is dying down and constraints start to feel negative, like being trapped. Keeping dedication alive is the secret of a successful marriage or relationship. Everything depends on dedication.

Dedication essentially means being a couple and having a future together. The first sure sign of dedication is a strong sense of identity as a couple. Kate and I show this by talking about ourselves as a couple. We think of ourselves as a couple. We do things together. We use the language of a couple, more "us and ours" than "you and yours" and "me and mine". We use a joint bank account and joint savings. We look after different household responsibilities on behalf of each other as a couple. For example, I sort out our household finances and our tax returns, and she sorts out our children's clothing.

The second sure sign of dedication is our sense of future together. This ranges from thinking, talking, and planning what we're going to do in the summer holidays or next Christmas, to where we see ourselves in ten years' time, to how we will spend our time together when the children have left home. Having a sense of future together also means that we are profoundly interested in each other's physical and mental health and well-being and are supportive of each other's hopes, dreams, and ambitions.

The third sure sign of dedication is that we put each other first. This means spending time together to make sure our friendship stays fresh and alive. When there is a clash of priorities, even with the children, then our marriage comes first. Putting each other first also means being prepared to let things go. We are both willing to lose an argument because the relationship is more important. It can sometimes take a while for either of us to back down, but we always do eventually. It would be pretty stupid and destructive to win the argument at the expense of the relationship. Forgiveness plays a key role in this. Holding on to the things that hurt us simply introduces a barrier – we have to let things go. We put each other first.

The fourth sure sign of dedication is willingness to sacrifice or give up other choices. If I choose to spend time with you, then I must be giving up the choice to spend time elsewhere. So when the opportunity arises to spend time elsewhere and I choose not to take it, it is showing sacrifice for the sake of the relationship. I'm not talking about being trodden on and treated as a doormat. I'm talking about going out of the way for one another: missing out on that social evening with work colleagues or that Saturday golf game with friends because we badly need time together; travelling home from a work trip late at night instead of staying over; putting my own work on hold in order to help out with a project that needs my support.

The reason I know for sure that Kate is committed to me is because she shows loads of dedication. She clearly talks and acts with our best interests at heart, as a team. She often talks about our future together, the things we need to plan for and the dreams of what we will do when we're old. She definitely puts us first. I spot it straightaway when she does something in my love language. I know she is showing her love. I also know she always forgives me when I say something hurtful. It doesn't always happen immediately; sometimes we need to resolve the issue.

But she always forgives me, eventually. And I know that she gives up opportunities for the sake of our marriage. She put her own career and ambitions second to mine for many years while she had our children. I only hope I showed sufficient appreciation of her sacrifice and am repaying the compliment to her now that she has the opportunity and talent to rebuild her career running a cookery school.

Marriage is the ultimate expression of dedication. The whole point of getting married is to make it crystal clear that we are a couple who plan to stay together for life. Marriage is also the mother of all constraints! Getting married makes it crystal clear to us and everybody else – friends, family, other singles, the law, government – that we are a couple who plan to stay together for life. And despite the media focus on divorce, it is still the case that most marriages today can expect to last for life. Of course not all marriages work. Couples slide into marriage without ever really committing. Couples clash, or they lose their sense of dedication and drift apart. But for the vast majority, marriage is the best and most reliable way of expressing commitment in both its forms.

I know beyond doubt that I am committed to Kate. I made a decision long ago to spend the rest of my life with her, for better or for worse. I live out that decision every day. Being dedicated to her and being married to her is how I show my commitment. But that's also how I know beyond any doubt that Kate is committed to me.

Looking for signs of commitment

A friend of ours in her early twenties recently asked Kate and me for some advice. Her long-term friendship with a young South American man was blossoming into romance. But because he lived on another continent, they hadn't actually been able to see each other face to face for over a year. Their relationship had been conducted mostly through the internet. She now had an opportunity to move to his country to see whether they could make their relationship work in real life. Did we think this was a good idea?

For me, the very fact that she was asking the question suggested she knew this was a huge risk. On the one hand, follow her heart and have some fun. On the other, take a huge step into the unknown at huge risk to her and little risk to him.

Based on what I know of dedication and the importance of deciding for men, my advice was simple. Normally I'd suggest looking for signs that he is using the language of "we" and talking about their long-term future. But since she can't hear the tone and attitude behind the words, mere words are not enough. She needs to see the actions behind the words. Most importantly, don't chase him. It's not for nothing that traditionally women can only pop the question every four years on 29 February; it's because the man needs to show his decision-making ability. Yes, by flying to him, she might continue to fall madly in love and have a whirlwind romance, even get married and have children. But moving country and language means she needs to be sure of his commitment to her future. She needs to see some sort of evidence of sacrifice from him. He needs to come to her. If she moves to him, she is doing all the deciding. He could end up sliding through the romance without ever really making the decision to commit. She doesn't have to break off the relationship, but she does need to look for a sign that he is willing to sacrifice for her.

I really should be an agony aunt.

Where to go for further help on relationships

If you're struggling with your marriage, relationship, or parenting, then allow me to make some practical suggestions that might make a big difference.

First of all, it's completely normal to have problems and arguments. I know some lucky couples claim never to argue. But if you talk together, you're going to highlight differences between you. Some of the time you're going to handle those differences well and some of the time badly. The vast majority of couples do go through difficult times together, especially when their children are young. But the vast majority of them also find ways to come through the tough times together. My marriage has come through more problems than most, so I know there are ways through. Having said that, I'm not about to pretend all marriages end up happily – they don't. Given the tendency of the media to focus on the bad news stories of the minority, it's easy to overlook the everyday good news stories of the majority. Contrary to popular belief, most UK couples marrying today will stay married for life, especially those in first-time marriages. Amazingly, almost all parents who stay together until their child is aged sixteen are married.[10] Very few successful long-term relationships exist outside marriage. In the USA, most people who say they are *unhappily* married report that they are *happily* married (to the same person!) five years later.[11] Even in countries like Malta, where divorce is legally difficult and socially frowned upon, married people are less likely to be distressed than in countries like the USA, where unilateral divorce is relatively easily available. All this says a lot for the durability of marriage.[12] So hang in there. You'll probably figure a way through together.

Second, it may seem a scary idea, but it's actually incredibly helpful to sit down and talk with a couple who have been through the difficulties that come with parenthood. Any older couple with children knows exactly what it's like to be new parents. They know the huge pleasure of bringing a new life into the world, but they also know how utterly exhausting it is. They know the strains it can put on new parents. Most importantly, they know that parenting comes in phases. Sleep-filled nights will return because children get older. Exhaustion may be today's challenge; tomorrow's will be the physical strain of lifting and shifting babies and paraphernalia. Later on, it will be the mental challenge of a six-year-old who won't sit down at supper, or an eleven-year-old who won't do their homework, or a fifteen-year-old who wants to sleep over with friends you don't know. Throughout it all are the magic moments when the family bonds, when faces relax and smile together, when a child says something touching and unexpected. Older couples know how this journey is worth sharing together as a couple. So be brave. Ask yourselves to dinner with older friends or extended family. They'll probably be honoured that you seek their advice. They may give you a few wacky ideas you'll need to disregard, but you'll also get experience and wisdom.

Third, think about going on a marriage and relationship course. You've read *Let's Stick Together*. This is simply a condensed version of the best available courses. The prospect may seem daunting and unfamiliar, but at the best courses, you don't have to speak, except to each other. You don't have to do any embarrassing group work. All you'll do is learn principles that work and, as a couple, discuss privately how they work for you. Once upon a time, antenatal or postnatal courses must have seemed a weird idea. Why do you need to learn about having a baby? It's natural, isn't it? Yet now antenatal and postnatal courses are very much the enjoyable and helpful norm for many couples. A modern relationship course will cover subjects such as commitment, conflict, and communication. Great marriage and great relationships can be learned. The principles are common for all of us.

Fourth, think about any serious individual issues. Sometimes one person will have personal issues that make a fruitful relationship extremely difficult. Alcoholism would be one obvious example. Mental health issues are another. Most commonly amongst new mums, it will be postnatal depression. Although postnatal depression can be a symptom of relationship problems or lack of involvement from the father, it may also be a chemical imbalance in the brain. The ideas in *Let's Stick Together* will definitely help if it's a relationship issue, but a visit to the doctor is a good idea in any case.

Fifth, if all else fails, by all means look up your local counselling organization.[13] Do this as a last resort, and make sure you go armed with a health warning. Many therapists and counsellors claim to take a neutral stance on marriage. They may tell you they are there to help people, not marriages. Therefore they will offer to help you work out the best solution for yourselves as individuals. This could leave you feeling pressured into making a false choice: between a happy divorce or an unhappy marriage.[14] But you are more than two individuals – you are a family. Your choice is neither divorce nor unhappiness. It is to make your marriage and family work. What you want is a counsellor who supports you in that goal and who will show you how to achieve it. Fortunately there are plenty of counsellors who do take this more optimistic and hopeful position. Just be sure to make things clear before you start: I want my marriage to work, and I want you to show me how.

Let's stick together!

CHAPTER SIX

Helping Yourselves Stick Together

I hope you've enjoyed *Let's Stick Together* and found it useful. Probably the best way to put what you've learned into practice is to choose a couple of specific changes you'd like to make. Don't try to do too much. All of the behaviours reflect "my" underlying attitude toward "you". Bad habits highlight where I am treating you badly. Good habits highlight where I am treating you well. So just pick one STOP sign that you tend to use most often and decide to use it a bit less over the next week. See how your spouse or partner reacts. Also, ask your spouse what particular thing makes them feel really loved. Focus on using that love language once during the next week, and then see how they react. Maybe the best thing you can do is think about how you value or support one another as parents, or maybe you need to decide to book in time together as a couple one night next week. Whatever you do, start with one or two specific things. Write them down below to remind you.

_____

_____

_____

_____

_____

Bad habits

Which STOP sign do I catch myself doing most often?

SCORE POINTS	When I feel criticized or accused, do I tend to react by pointing the finger back? Do I change the subject? Do I blame? Do I escalate?
THINK THE WORST	When something positive happens, do I wonder whether there is more to it than meets the eye? Are they being nice for a reason? Am I in trouble? When something negative happens, do I wonder whether they are doing it on purpose? Are they out to get me or to wind me up?
OPT OUT	When I feel under pressure or accused, do I tend to close down or back away? Do I storm out? Do I stop listening?
PUT DOWN	When somebody does something I don't like or want, do I think they are being stupid? Do I roll my eyes? Do I tell them they are stupid? Do I feel contempt? Am I critical or dismissive of them?

First of all, I need to think about the kind of situation in which I will typically react using this STOP sign. Then, when I catch myself doing it, or about to do it, I can try to react differently and see what happens. (Watch the four STOP videos at www.letssticktogether.com.)

During the next week, the STOP sign I will try to do less often is…

_____

_____

_____

_____

_____

_____

Good habits

What is my spouse/partner's main love language?

TIME   Hanging out together? Having a coffee? Watching TV? Going to the theatre or some other event?

WORDS   Chatting together? Gentleness in my voice? Not being harsh? Using compliments? Being encouraging?

ACTIONS Doing things together, such as games, sports, adventures, or DIY? Other activities? Doing things for one another? Helping with the baby? With household chores? With things that he/she would otherwise have to do themselves?

GIFTS   Always thinking about the other and buying

them little things? Sending them cards or
little notes?

TOUCH   Holding hands? Touching shoulders? Being
physically close?

First of all, I need to ask my spouse/partner what their love
language is. I'm not going to assume. My assumptions
might be completely wrong! So it's worth the check. "What
specific thing makes you feel really loved?"

During the next week, the specific love language I will
use at least once is...

_____

_____

_____

_____

_____

_____

What does dad do with the baby that makes mum most
frustrated, nervous, or critical? What does dad not do
with the baby that mum would like him to do more or do
better?

As a mum: Do I occasionally find myself treating dad
like an idiot? Do I need to trust him more when he is
with the baby? Does it really matter if he does things
differently? Do I need to show him a better way of
doing things? Do I need to encourage him that he is a
good dad?

As a dad: Do I support mum with the baby? Do I

react badly if she grabs the baby and says I'm doing it wrong? Do I need to learn not to take it so personally? Do I need to be more communicative if I'm nervous or unsure what to do? Do I need to ask for help if things are going wrong? Do I need to be a bit more forward in asking how I can help mum?

As a couple: Are we making time for each other? Are we having fun together? Has the baby taken centre stage in our lives so that we seem to have no time for each other? When we do have time off, do we tend to use it more to switch off, watch TV, relax in a bath, or have a rest? When did we last have a really good chat together?

During the next week, what I will do differently for mum/dad as a parent is…

_____

_____

_____

_____

_____

_____

During the next week, we will book in a date with one another on (day/time) to do (what) together…

_____

_____

_____

_____

_____

_____

Things they don't teach you in antenatal class
Which of the following do I want to apply in my family?

- Maybe we could start a family quote book or at least get one ready and waiting for when the comedy begins!
- Maybe we could think about building some of our own special family rituals for birthdays, holidays, Christmas, or other occasions.
- Maybe we could invent some family mottos of our own.
- Maybe we could discuss what we think about dad taking responsibility for family problems.
- Maybe we could discuss together exactly what dad's mission could be.
- Maybe we could discuss the decision we have made as mum and dad to enjoy family life together for the foreseeable future.
- Maybe it would be good to talk about how we show our commitment to one another and why we know we are committed, as a couple with a future.
- Maybe we need to have dinner with some older, wiser parents, whether friends or extended family, to chat through some of the relationship or family issues that challenge us. Maybe we could benefit from doing a relationship course or a parenting course together, to learn or remind ourselves of simple things each of us can do to make our family stronger.

During the next week, it would be good to chat about...

_____

_____

_____

_____

_____

Appendix
Helping Others Stick Together

The three main ideas in *Let's Stick Together* are all easy to understand, easy to apply, and easy to explain. I hope you feel this book has strengthened your own relationship and equipped you to help others too. If you fancy taking the message further, this chapter is for you. Many are intimidated by the idea of "teaching" other people about relationships. But don't let anyone insist you need to be an expert – you don't. Experience is what counts here. If you can relate to these ideas personally, explain how they work for you in real life, and manage a small group of parents, then you are ready to do more than tell your friends about it – you can spread the news further and help many new parents stick together.

You don't need to be an expert to teach others

I and my team of parent volunteers teach *Let's Stick Together* as a single session on relationships to dozens of antenatal, postnatal, and parenting groups in my home town of Bristol. My volunteers are ordinary intelligent parents who want to help support younger couples starting out. As parents themselves, they have experienced the effect babies and young children can have on the mum–dad relationship. They know at first hand how the principles in *Let's Stick Together* can make a big difference.

Teaching and learning about relationships is not rocket science. If you are a parent yourself and can explain these ideas and how they work for you to a small group of other parents, then you could easily run a session yourself. The principles in *Let's Stick Together* are based on careful research, so you don't need to be an expert. Think of people who have helped you most with family life. Often it's friends or family telling you how they experienced the same problem but found a way through. Research on longer relationship courses shows that ordinary lay educators do just as good a job as professionals.[1] So you don't have to know the answer to everything. You just need to be able to explain the principles and how you put them into practice. It's not your expertise that matters; it's your experience.

Nor do you need much training, if any at all. It only takes between forty minutes and an hour to deliver *Let's Stick Together*. The three key requirements are an understanding of the principles that you are teaching, a supply of relevant examples of how you use these principles in your own family life, and the ability to explain all this reasonably clearly to a group of people. If you've run other courses or groups, you may not need any training at all. As long as you have a practice run or two beforehand in front of friends at home, you'll find it fairly straightforward. If you haven't run courses, I recommend you watch the course in action and see how things are done. Watching somebody else will give you ideas about how it flows and what might or might not work for you. Just don't pretend to be somebody that you're not. Your credibility and your value depend on your experience and not your expertise. If you are interested in getting involved, please visit www. letssticktogether.co.uk.

What parents say about *Let's Stick Together*

Let's Stick Together goes down extremely well with both parents and group organizers, such as health visitors. We asked 404 mothers what they thought of their session. 70% of the mothers were married, 24% cohabiting, and 6% single/other. This is what they said:

- 94% said it was both "enjoyable" and "informative".
- 93% said it was neither "embarrassing", "boring", nor "scary".
- 94% (single mums as well) said the entire session was "useful".

Typical comments include:

- "The most useful session of our postnatal course!" (married mum)
- "Very eye-opening" (cohabiting mum)
- "Brilliant. Wish we had more time. Thank you" (single mum)

References

Chapter One

1. This is a brand new finding I made to accompany this book. Three big national surveys – the Census, Families and Children Study (FACS), and British Household Panel Survey (BHPS) – all show that 40% of British fifteen-year-olds no longer live with both natural parents. According to the 2001 census, almost all of the parents who stay together this long are married. Just 3% are not married. See my briefing paper under 'Research' at www.bcft.co.uk.

2. Although background factors – such as age, income, education, benefits, and ethnic group – influence the odds of new parents splitting up, the single biggest factor is whether the parents are married or not. Stephen Mackay of Birmingham University and I analysed data from the Millennium Cohort Study of 15,000 mothers who gave birth during 2000 and 2001. We found that across all income and education groups, unmarried parents with under fives were at least twice as likely to split up compared to equivalent married parents. This recent finding is part of the background research I made for my 2009 paper "Back off or fire back?" page 56, available as a free download at www.relationshipeducation.info.

3. To read some papers by top US researchers Scott Stanley and Galena Rhoades on how and why relationship education works, go to www.relationshipeducation.info.

4. See "Back off or fire back?" page 62.

Chapter Two

1. John Gottman of the University of Washington and his colleague Robert Levenson have showed that the best predictor of divorce during the early years of marriage is the presence of "negative affect" (criticism, defensiveness, contempt, and stonewalling) when discussing difficult issues. The best predictor of divorce during later years, as the couple's oldest child enters their teens, is the absence of "positive affect" (affection, interest, and humour) when discussing either everyday or difficult issues. In their words, "the absence of positive affect eventually takes its toll".

2. Gottman originally became famous for claiming to predict with 90% accuracy who will divorce and who won't in five years' time, simply by analysing a ten- or fifteen-minute video of the way couples talk to each other. This unlikely claim has now been thoroughly debunked. But the principle holds. How we treat each other today generally influences how we get on tomorrow.

3. The two most highly regarded marriage and relationship research groups in the USA both agree that the same sort of negative behaviours spell trouble for couples. Gottman calls them "The Four Horsemen". Howard Markman and Scott Stanley at the University of Denver call them "Danger signs". I call them STOP signs.

4. If you wish to read my whole study, it's called "Back off or fire back?" and you can download it for free from www.relationshipeducation.info.

Chapter Three

1. Although this won't be the case for everybody, many couples will definitely recognize themselves here. The negative aspects of marriage seem to be more important for men. The positive aspects seem to be more important for women. For example, Scott Stanley and colleagues at the University of Denver found that men's divorce potential is greater if they argue negatively, whereas women's divorce potential is greater if they are not treated positively (Family Process, 2002).

2. I highly recommend Gary Chapman's excellent and insightful book *The Five Love Languages*. Although I use a slightly different intepretation, the genius and simplicity of the idea is his.

Chapter Four

1. Researchers don't always agree on precisely how fathers and mothers influence both each other and their children. However, there is plenty of evidence that both parents play important and unique roles. Most people will find this blindingly obvious. Mums who feel supported are more likely to enjoy life. Children whose dads are involved are more likely to feel better supported and equipped for life. Even if it seems obvious, www.fatherhoodinstitute. org has some good research summaries if you want to read more on this surprisingly complex subject.

Chapter Five

1. Parenting can seem like a complex and confusing process. It's not. The principles of successful parenting are remarkably simple – love and

boundaries. Almost all researchers agree that the most successful parenting style, "authoritative", combines these two factors. Parents who only give love, and say yes, are "permissive" or "laisser-faire". Parents who only set boundaries, and say no, are "authoritarian". Children do best when they receive both love and boundaries, warmth and security, gentleness and firmness, yes and no. Watch those TV programmes when they send an expert in to help families with out-of-control children. The secret is almost always the introduction of whichever factor is absent, whether love or boundaries. That's the simple bit. The rest is technique. That's the hard bit. I did say the principles are simple, not the parenting itself!

2. I highly recommend *The Marriage Course*, *The Marriage Preparation Course* and *The Parenting Book*. They are all available worldwide through www.relationshipcentral.org.

3. I read *If Only He Knew* fifteen years ago. But author Gary Smalley's wisdom influenced me profoundly at a key moment when I was trying to understand why my marriage was in trouble and what I needed to do to make it work. A challenging read – but incredibly wise.

4. Both parents work in 56% of UK couple families with children under five (Office of National Statistics, Labour Market Review, 2005, page 276).

5. Only the father works in 34% of UK couple families with children under five, whereas only the mother works in 3% of these families (Office of National Statistics, Labour Market Review, 2005, page 276).

6. According to the 2001 census, there were 1.66 million lone mothers and 0.18 million lone fathers with dependent children in the UK (Focus on Families, 2007, page 4).

7. For further information, I encourage you to read about the biggest ever study into the effects of childcare by Professor Jay Belsky and colleagues in the 2007 *Child Development* journal. Or indeed, read any of his other recent articles on the subject.

7. This extraordinary finding by Galena Rhoades and colleagues in the *Journal of Family Psychology*, 2006, is the first clear evidence of "sliding, deciding, and inertia" theory put to the test.

8. Once again, I recommend a read of Scott Stanley and Galena Rhoades's article at www.relationshipeducation.info.

9. Yes, it's official: by looking at current and past rates of divorce, researchers Ben Wilson and Steve Smallwood project that 55% of UK couples marrying today will stay married (ONS, Population Trends, 2008, page 28). According to the 2001 census, 97% of parents who stay together until their child completes school are married. See my new briefing paper, 'New Statistics on Family Breakdown' under 'Research' at www.bcft.co.uk.

10. Using a large national sample in the USA, Linda Waite of the University of Chicago and colleagues found that two-thirds of unhappily married adults who avoided divorce or separation reported being happily married five years later. In a smaller accompanying study, she found that couples get happier for three main reasons: bad situations often improve over time anyway, couples decide to work at their marriage, or unhappy spouses change their lives in ways that make them personally happier ("Does divorce make people happy?", Institute for American Values, 2002).

11. Malta is one of only two countries in the world where divorce is illegal or difficult, the other being the Philippines. So if the bad news story about marriage is right, we should expect to find large numbers of Maltese couples trapped in unhappy or abusive marriages. However, Angela Abela of the University of Malta has found that 20% of married Maltese people are distressed at any one time compared to 32% of married people in the USA. You can read her paper at www.relationshipeducation.info.

12. Counselling can definitely be helpful, but it's not how most people turn their marriage around. Linda Waite's study says this: "Of the minority who went to counseling, most reported it was helpful, but relatively few saw it as the key to turning their marriages around or avoiding divorce."

13. In the same study, three-quarters of the people who said they were unhappily married had spouses who said they were happy! So it's mostly people that are unhappy, not marriages. Knowing this, it is less surprising to discover that the unhappily married adults who divorced or separated were no happier, on average, five years later than unhappily married adults who stayed married.

Appendix

1. A 2004 study by Jean-Philippe Laurenceau and colleagues in the *Journal of Consulting and Clinical Psychology* followed over 200 couples who had completed a pre-marriage relationship course. The couples whose course was led by non-expert community leaders did as well, and even better on some measures as the couples whose course was led by expert university-trained staff.